DATE DUE

DEC 14 1986 RET

MANAGING OFFICE SERVICES

MANAGING
OFFICE SERVICES

George R. Terry, (Ph.D.)

Consultant in Management
Chicago, Illinois

1966

Dow Jones-Irwin, Inc.

Homewood, Illinois

First printing, July, 1966
Second printing, April, 1969

LIBRARY OF CONGRESS CATALOG NO. 66–24595
PRINTED IN THE UNITED STATES OF AMERICA

INTRODUCTION

OFFICE services always have been, are now, and will continue to occupy a key position in office work performance. They are the oldest and, most likely, the best known of activities identified with the office. If there is nothing else, there must be office services present for an office, as we know it, to exist. There is always, for example, correspondence to write; mail to open, sort, and deliver; and papers to file. This work is ever present and is basic in every office and in every enterprise. In the great forward strides of the office, significant changes have occurred within this important office services area and more changes are on the way. The recognition of the fundamental importance and the universality of office services suggests as well as justifies a modern helpful volume covering this important phase of management applied to the office.

Managing Office Services is concentrated on identifying these vital services, describing the latest developments taking place within them, and suggesting practical ways in which they can be managed effectively. The dominant theme is that certain services provided by the office are essential to the entire enterprise, and these essential activities should be accomplished at the best time, place, and cost whereby they supply the maximum assistance to their recipients. This means that the dynamics—new thinking, new means, and new accomplishments of office services—should be incorporated into our present picture and concept of these particular office activities.

This book emphasizes the informative, how-best-to-do-it viewpoint. It not only tells how, but it also gives examples and many helpful guides. But it does not stop there because the ultimate goal is the *managing* of these services, and it is this phase of the material that is stressed and pointed out in a forthright manner so that most effective accomplishments can be gained. All the latest fabulous developments in the area of office services are included and their significance clearly indicated. The objective has been a thoroughly modern, complete yet concise, usable book. Illustrative material has been generously used to expedite understanding and to increase interest.

The book is intended to be profitable for anyone interested or engaged in office work. Included are the manager, staff assistant, supervisor, group leader, office employee, instructor, or student. They can be in a large,

v

medium, or small office or factory. And the enterprise can be one in business, education, government, military, or hospital. The broad activities of office services—corresponding, duplicating, retaining records, and handling office supplies—are common activities. Poorly done, they throttle the services provided by the office and therefore are worthy of competent management in every office.

The growth and the many changes of office work during the last several decades have tended to place developments such as the use of the computer, systems design, new office machines, and office methodology in the limelight. There is no question that all of these are important. But remaining in the background, given little fanfare, yet fundamental to everything done in the office and the "reason-to-be" for most office work are the office services. In no sense have these been replaced, nor their assistance rendered unneeded, by utilizing the more sophisticated approaches and techniques available today. The office remains essentially a service unit, and viewing what is done by the office from the office services viewpoint represents a basic and effective line of inquiry in improving office work. Pertinent questions to be answered include: What office services will be bettered? Who will benefit from these improvements? How do the contributions of these newer office services expedite the proper and planned operations of the entire enterprise? Information to answer such questions and to discuss them fully are included in this volume.

The material is arranged logically in *Managing Office Services*. Care has been taken to use clear expressions, to present key ideas, and to emphasize the truly important. Current effective practices have been given priority. The endless alternatives and the long descriptions of special situations have been reduced to a minimum. What is modern, what is effective, what is helpful, and what is practical have been included.

Nine chapters are offered. The first two concern the work of office writing. This includes the preparing of correspondence, memos, notices, messages, and reports. Chapter 1 emphasizes the challenge and the opportunity of office writing while Chapter 2 stresses the actual writing accomplishment—formats to follow, ideas to explore, developing writing skill, and adopting a purposeful writing style. Next, Chapter 3 deals with office communicating services and their proper use—the telephone, the telegram, personal messenger services, and paging services. Handling the office mail both incoming and outgoing is then discussed in Chapter 4. Zip coding, the latest in meter-mailing, and pertinent post office regulations including proper postage under current schedules, are among the subjects handled. Chapter 5 is titled "Duplicating." When, where, and how should copies of office papers be made? What processes are available and which one should be used where? Is an office printing shop feasible? Duplicating along with office communicating services represent two of the most rapidly changing activities in the entire office field. In Chapter 6, the work of calculating and comparing are set forth. In almost every office, calculating and comparing are performed—they are basic in office services. Next, filing is thoroughly discussed. An office is expected to retain written information for future possible use. For this purpose many filing arrangements and types of equipment are available. Supplying the information when requested, be it for a decision, contract, obligation, or transaction is essential to the effective conduct of the enterprise. But written information cannot be retained forever in the file. This brings up the subject of Chapter 8, or records retention, which includes deciding which papers to retain from the mass of those filed, and which to discard, so that adequate and satisfactory service at a reasonable cost is provided. Lastly, in Chapter 9, the handling of office supplies is presented. What supplies should be on hand, what costs should be incurred, where should the storeroom be located, and how best can proper control be kept over office supplies, are typical of the questions answered.

I am indebted to many for help in preparing this book. Managers, clients, employees, associates, teachers, and students have contributed generously of their assistance. Discussing office services, sharing information, and exchanging ideas with them have been most stimulating. These practical and down-to-earth conversations and interviews have given me a new appreciation of the importance and the vital contribution of office services. I have tried to include this attitude and belief in the pages of this book and to do justice to their excellent suggestions and encouragement which are sincerely and most deeply appreciated.

Chicago
June, 1966   GEORGE R. TERRY

TABLE OF CONTENTS

CHAPTER ONE

MEETING THE CHALLENGE

OF OFFICE WRITING

*Language was given us that we might
say pleasant things to each other.*
—Christian Bouce

Essential to the existence of every enterprise is the ability to organize and express ideas in writing. Adequate facility with the written word is required in our present world. Basic to office services is office writing and especially that dealing with letters and reports. No matter how proficient an executive managerially, an engineer technically, an office employee productively, his full worth is not revealed until he writes his suggestions and ideas interestingly and convincingly. Words are required to move men; words are basic in supplying necessary information. Like anything of value, words should be selected with care. One can select and arrange words to convey information clearly and accurately thus inducing effective action. In contrast, other words written in a communication can produce nonsense and misunderstanding and bring about unwanted action.

In this discussion the focus will be on corresponding and report writing. These are present in every office, and paper work even in its most limited concept always includes letters and reports, for these are the common media for keeping interested persons, both within and without the enterprise, informed on important matters.

CHALLENGE OF WRITING

One of the most powerful factors in the world is helpful ideas in the minds of energetic men of good will, presented to others in writing so that they can understand and use them. Writing presents a tremendous challenge. Skill in effective writing can be developed. It is not an ability with which some men are blessed and which others can never hope to achieve. Writing can be stimulating and it is a powerful tool. It can win men's hearts to a stated cause; it can distribute knowledge; it can implement effective action. A person you have never seen will change his course of action, send an inquiry, or start a new program—as a result of a letter or a report. This should inject a pride of accomplishment in writing really good letters and reports, and inspire one to be satisfied with only the best.

Office writing is not an awesome task. Too many view it as a difficult chore. There are simple methods to follow and with sincere practice the skill of writing can be achieved. Certainly, office writing should be clear, concise, complete, and cheerful. But above all else it must be useful. The information conveyed should be beneficial to the reader, should make his immediate task easier, facilitate his future efforts, or motivate him in ways favorable to him. And to be useful, information must be understood. Getting the message across as intended is vital. This means that care must be taken by the writer to make sure that his readers can plainly understand his writing. He does not take things for granted. Yet he realizes that the reader "must stretch" a little to comprehend the writing, otherwise the written words are simply conforming to beliefs and bits of knowledge the reader already has.

Many feel that there is too much writing in business today. They are correct. The difficulty is twofold: (1) writing unnecessary papers and (2) writing necessary papers ineffectively. The solution to the former is to eliminate them by means of enforcing a thorough program designed to limit all office systems, procedures, and practices to essential papers and activities. This approach is sound and produces outstandingly good results. In any given case, its potential should never be overlooked. However, the second condition, writing necessary papers ineffectively, is of our immediate concern. And this is directly related to recognizing the challenge of writing and taking proper steps to master it.

In addition to what has already been stated, one of the biggest challenges of office writing is to avoid being overimpressive. Some erroneously write to impress, they subconsciously seek to demonstrate the depth of their fund of knowledge. They seek to cover every facet of the subject and with a note of finality. What such writers forget is that the written words are a communication; they are to get ideas across, to provide requested information, and *to help the reader*.

SHORTEN AND PERSONALIZE THE WRITING

In nearly all cases, more effective office writing can be won by making the writing (1) more compact and (2) more personal. Much office writing is too wordy and too rambling. Excess words, vague meanings, and poor sentence structure characterize many office letters and reports. Conciseness and brevity should be sought. Many office letters are at least 35 percent larger than they need be. Abraham Lincoln's Gettysburg Address has less than 300 words, over two thirds of which are one syllable. The Ten Commandments are only 297 words. Certainly it should not require 500 words for a simple matter such as telling a customer his order has been delayed, the reason, and the revised shipping date.

And some sentences do not convey the meaning intended. To illustrate, in a letter of instructions to participants this warning was included, "We draw your attention to the fact that while in the clubhouse or on the courts, players must wear tennis shoes only." And the notice on the employees' bulletin board, "For Sale—Piano bench, like new, by billing clerk with carved legs." This is a variation of the newspaper want ad, "Experienced hostess, must be under 35 and respectable until after Thanksgiving." And a personnel manager in stressing help by the husband for his wife stated, "Acquire the habit of helping your wife. When she washes the dishes, wash the dishes with her; when she mops up the floor, mop up the floor with her."

The office writer must learn to look over his writing for sentences and words that he can omit. In a letter, for example, don't recapitulate the statements of the incoming letter. The sender knows what he wrote. A statement such as, "Your letter of August 22 in which you state that three dozen No. 10 fasteners were sent . . . ," usually can be eliminated.

Remember a letter writer doesn't answer letters; he answers people. Retain this personal touch in your writing. It is effective to use the addressee's name when it can be included naturally. For example, "It was a pleasure to have you visit our office, Mr. Smith." Adding this personal touch is effective. Likewise using the opportunity to write something more personal should be developed. To illustrate, "We are in receipt of your suggestion," becomes "Thank you for your suggestion."

Fortunately, we have a common written language, a condition not existent in some newly developed countries where each tribe has its individual and somewhat limited means of written communication. We have the means to write to each other in complete clarity and understanding. Our written language grows daily in size and complexity primarily because of new technology and custom. New words are coined and old words are assigned unique meanings. Yet, words well chosen and utilized generate interest and convey the specific information perfectly. What a waste of effort to write and not be understood.

SOME EXAMPLES

Let's look at a couple of examples of ineffective office writing. Suggested improvements will also be included. Here's a quotation from a letter of a large company:

It is understood that unless we make written objection within sixty days from the rendering of any bill for merchandise received, such bill shall be conclusive as to the correctness of the items and prices therein set forth and shall constitute an account stated.

With effort the intended meaning of this statement can be drawn from this statement. But the writing is difficult to comprehend, is not in a friendly tone, and precise words are missing. How might it be improved? The following is suggested:

Unless we complain about a bill within 60 days, it is accepted as is.

Another example dealing with advertising materials sent to a publisher:

When materials such as cuts, electrotypes, mats, and so forth received by us from the advertising agency occupy more space than specified in the insertion order, we will communicate with the agency for definite instructions. In the event that we cannot secure definite instructions, we will so notify the agency and follow the agency's subsequent instructions.

This can be briefed and made more direct by the agency stating:

If any material we send you is too big for the space specified, let us know immediately. We'll try to get definite instructions to you, otherwise, omit the advertisement.

READING

It is appropriate to discuss near the beginning of this chapter on office writing the subject of reading. Why is this? Because the writings of others must be read for communication to take place. We cannot write the answer to a letter until we read the letter to which we are replying. The report cannot be written until we read the information and research data that are to be included in that report. Reading is a basic tool and skill in it should be mastered if proficiency in office writing is to be attained.

Reading is the process by which man germinates ideas. The office writer's feel for "what to say" comes mainly from thoughts, requests, and information expressed in communications received and in stated or assumed policies and practices of his work area and environment. Reading is the copartner of writing. It would be more appropriate to term the office writer, the office reader and writer.

To write well it is therefore essential to read well. How best to do this has been subjected to much study and research. There is no one cardinal set of rules to follow, but the following are helpful and are recommended:

1. *Scan the material first.* Get the general notion of what it is all about by a fast searching scrutiny.

2. *Concentrate on the reading.* Eliminate mental and physical distractions that divide your attention and permit only partial effort to the immediate reading task.

3. *Read quickly.* Read in phrases or lines, not by words. Slow reading permits your attention to wander. Take a course in speed reading if you find reading is a time consuming chore.

4. *Spot the essential points.* Get the essence of what the material contains. The essential points provide the framework or backbone of the writing. The details or "fat upon the bones" can be obtained as the need for it arises.

5. *Increase your vocabulary.* Knowing the meaning of the words is basic to comprehending the material being read. There are over 500,000 words in the English language, but the average college graduate recognizes only 70,000 words. For ordinary business writing a mere 8,000 words will usually suffice, so the task of acquiring a suitable vocabulary is not especially difficult.

CLASSIFYING LETTERS AND REPORTS

Efforts to classify letters and reports into major types help to identify them and to designate the main purpose of each communication. Such information can be helpful in managing this area of office services.

Letters can usually be classified into those dealing with complaints, employment, purchasing, sales, or credit. In turn, letters in each of these major groups can be segregated further, as illustrated below.

Complaints—the replies are usually of four types:

1. Acknowledgment of complaint and promise to investigate and report later.

2. Adjustment of complaint, giving date and amount, and thanking addressee.

3. Refusal to adjust complaint, with reasons explaining why.

4. Request that the goods be returned for inspection and advise that further consideration will be given.

For *employment*—three types of replies are generally given:

1. Acknowledgment of application, stating that there is no opening at present.

2. Acknowledgment of application and request to report for work.

3. Welcome to newly hired worker of the company and explanation of company policies.

Reports can be classified into many different types, including private, public, company, departmental, restricted, nonrestricted, technical, and nontechnical. However, for purposes of office usage, the three groups of executive, periodic, and special are quite satisfactory. Under each of these classifications are the following:

Executive reports stress broad concepts and results rather than details, usually covering a three-, six-, or twelve-month time period. For the most part, they are prepared for members of top and intermediate management levels. They include (1) balance sheet, (2) statement of cost of goods sold, (3) statement of profit and loss, (4) budgetary statement, (5) annual departmental report, and (6) report to stockholders.

Periodic reports deal mainly with departmental activities and typically cover weekly, monthly, or quarterly periods. Usually some detailed information pertinent to the operation of the particular department is included. Periodic reports include (1) monthly reports on operation, (2) departmental records of performance, (3) monthly credit reports, (4) purchasing reports, (5) material-handling reports, (6) salesmen's reports, (7) advertising and sales promotion reports, and (8) personnel management reports.

Special reports cover activities not covered by other reports. They are published at frequent intervals and include subjects such as product development, marketing research, plant location, company insurance and pension revisions, and various projects of a nonrecurring nature. A portion of a special report dealing with the findings of a market research study is shown in Figure 1.

ORGANIZING THE CONTENTS OF A LETTER

An effective letter starts by telling the reader what the letter is all about. This can be done in a number of ways such as an "attention of" line, a subject heading at the top of the letter, or an inclusive statement in the opening sentence. The point is that the reader should not have to guess what the subject is or be permitted to lose his interest in the letter by not being immediately informed of the subject. To illustrate, a good opening is, "Yes, you are entitled to an adjustment in our billing of April 3."

The main content, or body, of the letter should be arranged so it is easy for the reader to follow. Start with what the reader knows and lead him to the unknown. Or give the reasons before stating the decision or news itself—this approach has a strong element of persuasion about it. Some

35–E   X Research Company   N 58

SUMMARY OF FINDINGS

OBJECTIVE:

To obtain a measure of consumer acceptance of Product Y.

RESULTS:

1. Product Y is not as well liked as Product No. 17.
2. The market potential of Product Y is somewhat between 50% and 80% of the market for Product No. 17. These are the limits indicated by consumers' stated preferences and test-package consumption.
3. The preference for Product No. 17 over Product Y prevails in all geographical areas and among all types of consumers. The greatest liking for Product Y was found among women.
4. Product No. 17 is preferred chiefly because it is crisp, easy to eat, and has a sweet, mild flavor.
5. Product Y is preferred by those who like a harder and heavier cereal than Product No. 17. Most cold cereal users, however, thought Product Y too hard to chew.
6. While food value is not a dominant factor in consumers' preferences between cereals, Product Y was the choice of consumers who emphasize this point.

CONCLUSION:

There is a limited market for an expanded cereal that is harder and heavier than Product No. 17. The potential volume of one such cereal—Product Y—is between 50% and 80% of the Product No. 17 market.

FIG. 1. A portion of a special report.

advocate following a "logical format," by which is usually meant a chronological approach. Many times this is effective, but it should not be followed blindly. In some instances, including only the current or latest information is satisfactory and in other cases the reverse of chronological, or starting with the present and working back to the beginning, is superior.

The close should be just that, the close. It needs to be specific and definite. The reader should not have to second guess what the answer or reply is. When you reach the close, state it, and quit writing. Nothing is more ineffective than a letter which contains a closing, then continues to another closing and after several of these potential closures, states an abrupt "Sincerely yours."

Tone is an important consideration in organizing a letter. By tone is meant that public relations ingredient that commonly determines whether as a result of the letter the reader is favorably inclined toward the writer or his company. An office letter writer holds a key position in shaping the public feeling toward his employer and the products or services provided. In effect, the letter writer helps to mold the personality of the company in the minds of the public. To gain proper tone, the writing should be friendly and reveal a concern for the reader's problem. Include courteous words and write in a natural, ordinary manner. Avoid the special jargon, stilted, and unusual expressions. Minimize the use of negative words; transform them into positive ones. For example, "We seek to avoid forgetting past due accounts . . ." has better tone when stated, "We try to remember past due accounts. . . ."

The so-called "No-letter" requires special care in organizing. The problem is to give a negative reply, but get the reader to see the justification for the refusal, and to retain his good will. Often a no-letter must be written under quite emotional circumstances. As stated above an effective opening and closing along with the proper tone are essential. However, the body of the letter can usually best be handled by first giving the reasons for the bad news and then stating the refusal itself. Conciseness is particularly important in the no-letter.

ADDITIONAL CONSIDERATIONS TO EMPHASIZE

Definiteness, correct spelling, and proper punctuation are additional considerations to emphasize in office letter writing. Reference to the particular subject, quotation, expenditure, or agreement is usually important and the statement should make the reference clear. Otherwise, the recipient's understanding of the statement may be different from that intended, thus giving rise to future difficulties. Vagueness can be very costly. Suppose a prospective buyer viewed two trucks on a seller's lot. The following day the buyer writes the seller, "I have decided to buy the truck that represents the greater value as indicated in our conversation yesterday." This surely will lead to disagreement. The writer has failed to state definitely the truck to which he is referring. Likewise, the sentence in a sales letter, "Our canned corn is the best on the market," is completely void of definiteness and may expose the writer to offering proof of such a statement in court. It is better to temper such all-inclusive statements by, "It is believed that," or "We feel that," so that the above controversial sentence would read, "We feel that our canned corn is the best on the market." Also, never quote another person unless you have his approval or know he approves fully of your doing so. To write, "Mr. Miller says you are going to modify your job evaluation program," is a dangerous statement to include in a letter unless you know Mr. Miller is authorized to release such information and Mr. Miller has approved the writing of such a statement. Furthermore, in the case of credit letters, do not state anything detrimental to the applicant's character. Stay with the facts but avoid writing opinions concerning a person's personal characteristics and behavior.

Letters containing incorrectly spelled words indicate sloppy work, lack of essential knowledge, and indifference to detail. Acquiring the ability to spell correctly is aided by reading. The one who reads a great deal ordinarily spells correctly. It is unreasonable to expect the writer to spell all words correctly, but he should know when he is not certain of the spelling and look it up in a dictionary. In the main, spelling ability is greatly influenced by experience and memory. Being exposed to a word frequently and using it from time to time aids in spelling that word correctly. There are spelling rules and these merit study even though there appear to be major exceptions to each one of them. However, memory, practice, and usage are the outstanding aids to spelling. Memory is probably the most important and hence, any weakness in spelling can be overcome through study. Figure 2 gives a list of often misspelled words. A glance over this selected list will indicate where you stand in spelling ability.

Punctuation is also important. The intended meaning and clarity of the communication are greatly assisted by proper punctuation. Compare the following statements:

High-speed cars do not stop on highway.
High-speed cars. Do not stop on highway.

And the following:

Do not break your crackers or roll in your soup.
Do not break your crackers, or roll, in your soup.

Figure 3 shows suggestions that will help in using proper punctuation.

ARRANGEMENT OF LETTER

A business letter should make a favorable first impression. To do this, it should be well placed on the page, have margins as even as possible, have a uniformity of typing or print, and give a clean and neat appearance.

There is probably no one best form for a business letter. Usually, a general pattern is in common usage; but slight variations are the rule, depending upon the particular needs and wishes of the writer. Most readers are accustomed to the general pattern and look for certain

accessible	facilities	pamphlet
acclimate	familiar	parallel
accommodate	financial	peculiar
accurate	foresight	perceptible
accustomed		permanent
admirable	genuine	persuade
advisable	guarantee	planning
affidavit		precede
all right	ignorant	preference
already	ignitible	proceed
apparatus	illegible	
arguing	immense	qualifications
ascertain	inaccessible	questionnaire
	inasmuch	
beginning	incessant	receive
believe	inconvincible	refrigerator
bulletin	indispensable	remittance
bureau	interpret	remunerate
	interrupt	repetition
cancellation	irrelevant	reversible
chargeable	irresistible	
collapsible	issuing	salable
collateral		scissors
committees	judgment	seize
comparatively	justifying	separate
comprehensible		serviceable
conscience	leisure	shipment
continuance	leniency	shipped
counselor	license	similar
criticism		subtle
	mailable	susceptible
deceive	masterpiece	
deductible	mediocre	tentative
desirable	mileage	textbook
dilemma	mischievous	transferred
docile		
	occasion	vehement
eligible	occur	vehicle
embarrass	occurrence	verify
equipped	omission	vicious
expressible	owing	viewpoint

FIG. 2. List of commonly misspelled words.

information in certain locations. Figure 4 shows the forms of several different types, including (1) indented paragraphs, (2) block paragraphs, and (3) simplified letter. The difference between indented paragraphs and block paragraphs is that in the latter the paragraphs are started at the left margin. In the simplified letter, all material starts at the left margin, the saluation is omitted—in its place the subject of the letter is written—and the complimentary close is omitted. Slight variations from these three forms of letters are employed. One large national distributor, for example,

THE PERIOD (.)
At the end of a complete declarative or imperative sentence.

Always inside of quotation marks.

To close a request.

THE COMMA (,)
To separate a series of words, phrases or clauses.

In a series of three or more nouns, adjectives, or adverbs, the last of which is connected by a conjunction (as well as a comma).

To set off the name of person addressed.

Before and after a nonrestrictive clause begun by "who," "which," or "that."

After words used to give emphasis in a sentence—for example, "oh," "no," "well," "therefore."

Before and after words in apposition.

For emphatic setting off of a part of a sentence.

THE COLON (:)
After the salutation in a letter.

To set off a lengthy quotation, statement, or list.

THE SEMICOLON (;)
To break up complicated sentences of unusual length which involve commas.

THE DASH (—)
To show a definite break in thought.

When repetition is used for emphasis.

THE HYPHEN (-)
In compound words—e.g., "featherlight," "an up-to-the-minute bulletin."

THE INTERROGATION POINT (?)
Always follows a direct question.

THE EXCLAMATION POINT (!)
Following a sentence or phrase, expresses emotion, surprise, or command.

THE APOSTROPHE (')
Signifies possession when coming before the "s" in possessive nouns.

Shows omission of letters in contractions.

To enclose a quotation within a quotation.

QUOTATION MARKS (" ")
To enclose a direct quotation.

To indicate a word that is defined.

FIG. 3.   A list of usable punctuation.

uses the block paragraph form with open punctuation, that is, commas and periods are omitted at end of date, address, and close.

In many instances the situation does not require a letter; a short well-written memorandum is adequate. Figure 5 illustrates an effective memorandum. Terse headings simplify the job of writing because they unify simple sentences into a condensed and informative message.

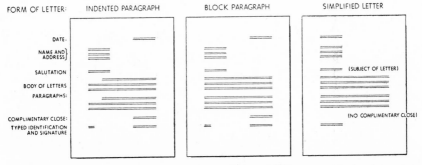

FIG. 4.   The respective forms of three different letters used in business.

April 25, 19—

To:	T. E. Miller
SUBJECT:	Storing purchased parts in our stores.
OBJECTIVE:	To reduce damage to parts while in transit or in stores.
SCOPE OF PROJECT:	Try to attain:
	1. Better package design and material.
	2. Improved physical inventory taking.
	3. Better utilization of stores space.
	4. Efficient housekeeping in stores.
TIME REQUIRED:	Approximately six weeks.
SUBMITTED BY:	J. D. Black

FIG. 5.   Example of an effective short memorandum.

SPEED LETTER

In order to simplify the work of correspondence, the so-called "speed letter" is used by many business writers. See Figure 6. In this letter, space is provided for a listing of recipients making up a mailing route, and preprinted information is included so that the appropriate information can be indicated by a simple check mark. Additional space is provided for such individual information as may be required.

A speed letter is a preprinted form designating certain spaces for filling in desired information. Commonly, three copies are made. The original is retained by the sender; copies No. 2 and 3 are sent to the receiver, who writes in his reply, returns copy No. 2, and retains copy No. 3. Some designs provide spaces for "From" and "To" at the top of the sheet and a line for the "Subject" to be written in, below which is a space for the "Message," and below it, the "Reply."

FORM LETTERS

As stated above, most letters can be classified into a relatively small number of types. This fact suggests and has led to letter standardization, or the use of form letters. A form letter is *a standardized letter which is used by an enterprise to answer all correspondence on a similar or recurring subject, or which is used to give the same information to many addressees.* A form letter may be sent to accounts past due. Such a letter, keyed "Delinquent Collection Letter No. 1," is sent to all accounts in arrears, with the appropriate name and address added at the top. After a certain amount of time, a "Delinquent Collection Letter No. 2" may be sent to those accounts which remain unpaid.

DEMPSTER CORP. CHICAGO, ILL. SPEED LETTER		DATE		
TO: 1	LOCATION		INITIALS	DATE
2				
3				
4				
5				
APPROVAL		NOTE AND FORWARD		
AS REQUESTED		NOTE AND RETURN		
COMMENT		NOTE ENDORST OF ACTION TAKEN		
FOR YOUR INFORMATION		PER CONVERSATION		
INITIAL FOR CLEARANCE		PREPARE REPLY		
NECESSARY ACTION		SIGNATURE		
MESSAGE				
SIGNATURE			TITLE	

FIG. 6. A well-planned printed form to expedite written communication.

The chief advantages in the use of form letters are that they (1) afford a uniform operation, (2) conserve both the dictator's and the typist's time, and (3) help reduce letter costs. On the other hand, there are disadvantages in the use of form letters, including: (1) They are not keyed to the requirements of individual cases, (2) they may be a little stilted, and (3) they are very often discounted by the receiver because of the lack of a personal touch.

Generally speaking, form letters serve a very useful purpose. They are tailored to fit certain conditions and are usually worked over by several correspondents to create the best possible results. They need not be impersonal, and it is not necessary to send the same letter again and again to the same customer. When they are properly handled, there should be no objection to form letters.

FORM PARAGRAPHS

Form paragraphs are similar in idea to form letters but apply to standardized paragraphs only. Under this practice, letters are composed of form paragraphs plus individual ones. Experts are frequently engaged to develop the form paragraphs.

It is customary for the dictator to use several variants of a form paragraph. This permits some diversity. The approved form paragraphs are listed, keyed, and indexed, and are made available to all correspondents.

DEVELOPING FORM LETTERS AND PARAGRAPHS

Form letters and form paragraphs can be "armchaired" from handy references, or they can be obtained by actual practice. The latter is recommended. To do this, simply take these steps:

1. For a period of four weeks, make an extra copy of every letter written.

2. At the end of this period, sort the copies by major subject and further by types under each major heading.

3. Determine the types of letters most frequently written and also, under each type, the most frequently used paragraphs.

4. Select the best reply to each frequently asked question and also the best expression of the necessary information.

5. Standardize these forms, and incorporate them as form paragraphs and form letters.

6. Repeat this entire procedure every 12 months; then, adjust and improve form paragraphs and letters as suggested by findings.

For this work, the office manager should enlist the services of all letter-writing people in his office. Participation will not only help win acceptance of the program of improving correspondence but will also utilize the best personnel for this work, raise morale, and increase efficiency.

FORMAT FOR REPORTS

There is no one best way to arrange the information of a report. In some instances, a standardized format is well established and accepted; but in many cases, the writer is free to choose the makeup. Material should be presented logically. Aids which will help in the reading should be provided—for example, simple statements, sectional headings, summaries at the beginning, and a table of contents. A reader often glances through a report, noting the various headings and reading a sentence here and there. For this reason, it is advisable to make it possible to obtain a "quickie" on what the report is all about and what it includes. This

PROCEDURE NO. 2

Subject: Retrieving Records from the Center

Performed By	Action
Department Records Clerk	1. When information is needed from an inactive record, phones Records Center.
	2. Refers to the returned copy of form PSC-418, TRANSMITTAL LIST - INACTIVE RECORDS. Gives the Records Center location carton number, folder, and document wanted.
Records Center Clerk	3. Asks inquirer if this information can be given by telephone.
	3a If phone answer is OK, goes to shelf location, retrieves record, and gives information wanted.
	VARIATIONS
	4. If information cannot be given by telephone, and requester wants entire record, asks if a copy will do.

PROCEDURE NO. 3

Subject: Destroying Inactive Records

Performed By	Action
Records Center Clerk	1. Checks destruction tickler file each month. Pulls out cards indicating the records which are scheduled for destruction.
	2. For each group (same form No. etc.) Fills out form PSC-435, DESTRUCTION NOTICE in 2 copies.
	3. Sends one copy to the department records clerk of the department of "basic interest."
Department Manager	3a. If, upon notice of scheduled destruction, d e c i d e s the group of records should be retained longer, fills out form PSC-445 RETENTION SCHEDULE REVISION.
Department Records Clerk	3b. Sends or takes form PSC-445 to Records Center clerk.
Records Center Clerk	3c. Retains records for an additional 30 to 90 days.

Courtesy: "Systemation Letter," Foundation for Administrative Research, Tulsa, Okla.

FIG. 7.   The effective "Playscript Procedure" is winning wide acceptance.

approach will maintain the reader's interest and lead him to correct conclusions and proper actions.

Every report should follow a carefully developed general outline. The first step in preparing such an outline is to select the information to be included in the report. This is ordinarily dictated by the purpose of the report, what information is available, or what can be uncovered. Next, the items of information should be classified under headings which normally are grouped as major and minor, or as many groups as judgment suggests.

The so-called playscript procedure is an effective format for writing. It clearly spells out who does what in a sequential order. Its use is rapidly spreading with wide impact. Figure 7 shows this arrangement.

Charts, drawings, pictures, and maps help to convey the meaning to the reader, but they must be carefully selected and employed in "reasonable" amounts for maximum effectiveness. In many cases, the chart or drawing must be explained and significant relations pointed out to the reader, because the exact meaning may not be gained simply by looking at the illustrative material. Pictures are especially helpful in dealing with technical subjects.

OUTLINES FOR REPORTS

There are a number of general outlines for reports; the following is preferred by many: (1) summary of findings, (2) methodology, (3) detailed results, and (4) appendix. Another outline which is effective and adaptable for many subjects, especially those of a technical nature, includes: (1) summary, (2) objective and scope, (3) equipment used, (4) methodology, (5) data obtained, (6) conclusions, and (7) recommendations. The following has also won favor: (1) introduction and definition of problem, (2) conclusions and recommendations, (3) discussion of procedure and results obtained, and (4) summary. Another is: (1) digest of findings and recommendations, (2) background of study, (3) savings and other benefits to be gained, (4) possible drawbacks, (5) alternatives and why choice of the one recommended, and (6) proposed implementation plan.

It should be observed that in each of these outlines, either the summary, conclusion, or recommendation is included near the beginning of the report. This may seem illogical; but actually it is not. The sequence of items need not be chronologic; however, there should be *some order* in presenting the material. The great majority of report readers want the gist of the findings or the conclusions right away, so it is effective to put this information at the beginning.

AROWI

Some report writers find the *AROWI* approach very helpful. *AROWI* stands for a five-step report-writing outline inclusive of the major considerations in this type of writing. The *A* means the Attitude of the writer, the *R* represents the Reader for whom the report is being written, the *O* means Organizing the material for the report, the *W* is for Writing the first draft, and the *I* indicates Improving the first draft through revisions. *AROWI* is complete and when faithfully followed assists in creating reports that produce highly favorable results.

Attitude of the writer, for example, represented by *A*, greatly conditions his efforts. His belief in the report and what it will include, in communicating with recipients of the report, and in writing to share information with the reader, establishes the entire mood and level of the writing. Improvement of writing style frequently begins with the writer examining his attitude. Does he visualize the reader when he sits down to write? Does he know for whom he is writing? Next, the letter *R* for reader, points out the real need for the writer to consider what readers are going to use the report and what data are required, the reader's scope of experience, the best way to present the information to the readers, and the possible reactions the readers should have. After checking his own attitude and considering the reader, the report writer is then ready for *O,* or organizing the material. This brings up the points to be covered, the sequence to be followed, the nature of the material, and arranging the main headings and subheadings. *W,* or writing the report follows. This includes all the ramifications in getting the facts, findings, and ideas down on paper. The type and tone of language must be developed and the whole writing made interesting and stimulating to the reader. Decisions as to where to use illustrations and charts are also reached. Finally, the *I* for improving the writing takes place. Included are a general evaluation of the report's contents, interpretation of information, sentence structures used, selection of words, writing style, avoidance of unnecessary repetition, irrelevancy, and hedging. Most reports are revised and rewritten in part; seldom, if ever, is the ideal writing achieved in the first draft.

CONSTRAINTS UPON REPORT WRITERS

It is helpful to place certain constraints over the efforts of report writers. While such action may result in certain losses, the over-all effect is to gain much more than is lost. Constraint No. 1 is to *require conformance in format as far as possible.* When most reports within an enterprise are so written, assimilation of the information is quickened. Insist that the conclusions or recommendations stand out. Have the arguments listed substantiating each conclusion and in the list note the evidence used to infer the conclusions made. By stripping down the logics and association of data in this manner, the report is easier to read and areas of differences can be quickly spotted. Constraint No. 2 is *demand more than one recommendation.* This makes for an exhaustive and thorough study. When only one recommendation is offered the decision is either "yes" or "no." In many instances, however, a portion of a single recommendation is considered very worthwhile, but another portion poses certain misgivings. Providing an option or two of what action might be taken expedites the decision making and also keeps the writer's thinking more flexible.

Practice exception reporting is constraint No. 3. What does this mean? It is the application of the old exception principle in management whereby only the exceptional matters are brought to the manager's attention. The ordinary situations continue to operate without the management member's attention. Exception reporting therefore is the practice of writing reports only when operations deviate a greater than predetermined amount from expectancy. These are the exceptional cases and reports on them provide pertinent information on situations that require attention. Constraint No. 4 is *insist on brevity*. Every subject and every problem can be summarized. Have the highlights identified and acquire comprehension of the "whole picture and its interrelated parts" by insisting that this big picture be presented concisely. Summary paragraphs, even summary sentences, are effective. More information can usually be obtained if it is needed.

GUIDES FOR EFFECTIVE BUSINESS WRITING

Specifically, what can be done to improve our business writing? How do you combat the conditions leading to writing wherein the ideas are jumbled, statements are ambiguous, the sentence structure is poor, and the intended meaning is camouflaged? Suggestions have been included throughout this chapter, but to reiterate and for convenience the following ten pertinent guides will help considerably and include:

1. *Make the writing serve a known and definite purpose.* In the case of letters, for example, know exactly what is to be accomplished by the letter. Settle on one main issue and concentrate on it. Letters pertaining to a single subject are easy to understand, and they expedite filing.

Reports are written to help the recipient and should be appropriate to the plan, decision, or directive about which he is concerned. It is essential that the aim of the letter or the report be known to the person preparing it because this knowledge guides the writer and helps him point the communication toward its intended uses.

2. *Keep the recipient in mind.* The aim of a letter or of a report stands a much better chance of accomplishment if its text is understood. To expedite this understanding, the needs, wants, and interests of the recipient should be given prime consideration. What a reader acquires from a written business communication is conditioned by the knowledge he brings to it. That is, a person who has broad training and an extensive background in a particular subject will acquire more from a report in that subject than the individual who does not possess such training and background. For this reason put the reader in the center of what is

written. Look at the subject from his viewpoint; visualize the reader while writing, and tailor the material and expressions to him.

In letter writing, for example, the technique of the "you viewpoint" can be followed. To illustrate:

Write:

"You may have quick service if you'll just telephone ORchard 1–7777."

Do not write:

"We wish to call attention to the fact that we are in the dry-cleaning business and have a 15-year record of excellent service. Our telephone number is ORchard 1–7777."

3. *Be factual and unbiased.* Accuracy is essential to good writing regardless of the scope, subject, medium, or level for which it is intended. The facts should be relevant to the subject; opinions should be identified as such. Irrelevant details should be excluded. What is basic to the stated purpose should be included. Information which is incomplete and not essential to the purpose should be avoided.

The motive and the ideas should be presented without bias. Stress the objective viewpoint. Fundamentally, the writing is being done to inform the reader of the situation or subject as it is. A letter or a report can be colorful, yet not filled with emotional statements. Remember that the content and the words should be tools of straight thinking, not stumbling blocks.

4. *Use short familiar words and simple sentences.* Word choice is vital; simple words are bold and clear and usually convey the intended meaning. Some writers never use a short, familiar word if they know a big one of similar meaning, and such practice weakens a letter or a report. Employing the word, "nonprofitization" instead of deficit and "pre-associated personnel" rather than former employee are examples of unusual words that hinder rather than help the communication. Employing words in common usage is a good rule to follow. This is well illustrated by a story about Benjamin Franklin. When still a lad, he told his mother: "I have imbibed an acephalous mollusk." His mother, believing young Franklin had swallowed something poisonous, forced him to take a large dosage of medicine to induce vomiting. When he got over the effects of the medicine, he explained to his mother: "I have eaten nothing but an oyster." Whereupon his mother thrashed him for deceiving her. Franklin later advised: "Never use big words when little words will do."

Clear sentences are one of the most helpful ingredients of clear reports. Although variety in sentence length is desirable, short sentences are normally preferred. Some say that no sentence should be longer than 25 words. However, it should be long enough to convey the thought. A practical suggestion is to fit the sentence to the reader's span of attention. Omit involved phrases, as well as those that are awkward or incorrect, and weed out the extra words. Tabulate lists for greater clarity. Unity, coherence, and correct sentence structure are more readily achieved in short than in long, complex sentences. Correct punctuation also helps.

5. *Employ active verbs.* Present-tense verbs create more interest and convey activity better than past-tense or subjunctive-tense verbs. "He understands" has more vigor than "It is understood by him" or "He should have understood." While some variation is desirable, try to use a good portion of active verbs in your writing. Also, choose the strong, virile verbs; avoid the weak ones. "Put the records into a single file" is stronger than "Gather the records and place into a single file."

6. *Use conversational style.* Letters and reports are communicative devices and are more readily understood when written in a style to which we are accustomed. We are familiar with the conversational style and from it quickly grasp the meaning. Ordinarily we do not use exotic words and long sentences with qualifying phrases in our normal speech. Why insist on using these communication blocks in our written work? Think of your writing as taking the place of a personal visit. The writing is really you making a call. This viewpoint will force you to write in a natural conversational style.

7. *Establish an acceptable mood.* Be friendly and let your writing reflect your own natural self. Letters and reports are written to human beings, not merely to names. Write naturally and humanly. Stilted, highly formalized statements are taboo. Avoid "whisker" expressions, examples of which, along with improvements, include

Do not use	*Use*
I am not in a position	I cannot
My attention has been called	I notice
Enclosed please find	We enclose
Has come to hand	Referred to me
Acquaint me with the facts	Tell me
Under separate cover	Separately
Contents duly noted	I have read
At this time	At present
We have reviewed our records	We find
It is our opinion	I believe
Take pleasure	Are pleased
We have yours of the 10th	Your letter of November 10

The top of Figure 8 illustrates a letter written in a stilted manner and using whisker expressions; an improvement is shown in the bottom portion of this figure.

March 15, 19--

Dear Sir:

    Your letter addressed to our Chicago plant has been referred to the undersigned for reply. We wish to advise that it is our long standing policy to limit our sales promotion efforts to ideas originating with our advertising agencies. Therefore, we cannot accept your suggestion.

    Enclosed herewith is your letter and under separate cover your display unit is being returned.

    Needless to say, we want to extend our thanks to you for your interest in our products and their sales.

                          Very truly yours,

March 15, 19--

Dear Mr. Hayes:

    Thanks for your suggestion concerning the display unit for our products.

    Our executive committee has decided not to change the current means of display. This was decided in view of our present sales and the costs for changing our sales program at this time. There are also some legal difficulties to which the use of this display unit might expose both you and ourselves. We would want to clarify these legal points before considering your suggestion for future action.

    We will keep you informed of developments.

                          Very truly yours,

FIG. 8. *Top:* A letter written in a stilted manner. *Bottom:* An improvement over the letter above.

When writing use a tone that wins cooperation or puts the reader in a mood to read the communication and give thought to it. Positive expressions help to accomplish this goal. Greater acceptance and motivation are gained by writing in an optimistic tone. For example, in a letter, write: "We can send you tickets for the November 27 performance," instead of "We cannot send tickets for any performance prior to that of November 27."

8. *Make the writing clear.* This requires knowing what must be included and in what sequence it should be presented. The writer should express each thought so clearly that the reader is certain to understand it. Normally, the transcriber helps in acquiring clarity by straightening out improper sentence structure and switching words. Remember too that proper punctuation helps make the writing clear and keeps the meaning from becoming ambiguous. A properly placed comma, semicolon, or period can do wonders in clarifying the meaning. It is well to have a competent person edit a report to insure that the meaning is clear.

Have your writing say exactly what you intend it to say, and mean what the writing says. These eight words form the basis of all great writing: "Write so that you cannot possibly be misunderstood."

9. *Interpret findings adequately.* Care must be exercised to avoid exaggeration or the inclusion of unqualified interpretations which cannot be reasonably derived from the available information. It is usually best to understate rather than to overstate conclusions. Also, recommendations must be practical and sound.

10. *Summarize briefly and make writing conclusive.* Normally, it is best to state the results in a summary statement. Convey the essentials to the reader easily; under no circumstances should the receiver be required to dig through quantities of words and figures to find out what the writing discloses or is all about.

Be certain to include what action, if any, is desired of the reader, what the writer will do, or what the writer wants done. Be decisive; let the reader know exactly the recommended course or disposition. Avoid double meanings. Long, qualified explanations usually offer little help. Strive to set forth the recommendations so clearly and effectively that they will be followed.

CHAPTER TWO

GETTING OFFICE WRITING

ACCOMPLISHED

Everyone has talent at twenty-five.
The difficulty is to have it at fifty.
—Edgar Degas

IN THE last chapter our interest centered mainly upon creating the office writing, making it effective, and employing proper words and sentence structure. Suggestions, examples, and guides were included to assist in achieving writing proficiency. We now shift our attention from the creative aspects to the mechanics of letter and report writing or the task of getting the office writing accomplished. Major topics to be included are the procedure to follow, the machines available, motivating the office writers, keeping writing costs within reasonable limits, and controlling the writing efforts.

PROCEDURE FOR HANDLING WRITING WORK

A definite procedure is required to handle the work of writing letters and reports; this cannot be left to chance. Relying upon haphazard methods to accomplish the work promptly is wishful thinking. The following is suggested:

1. *In the case of correspondence, get letters to those who answer them.* Letters on ordinary and routine subjects can be quickly routed to the proper party for reply. In contrast, letters dealing with out-of-the-ordinary subjects frequently offer some difficulty. Frequently, these letters are addressed to the wrong person within the enterprise and must be rerouted. The task of getting letters to the proper persons for answering is

usually the responsibility of the head of the mailing department or the office manager.

For reports, the subject area to be covered, time for completion of report, and designation of the writer are basic decisions to be made. In many cases, established policies regarding report writing guide the initial planning steps of report preparation.

2. *Get facts to the correspondent.* To write meaningfully, the writer must have all the facts. To write a sales letter, for example, one must have information on what the product will do, its good points, its price, and the like. Likewise, to compose a report requires access to pertinent information and some knowledge of the facts in the particular subject area.

When filed material is required in order to write a letter, it is obtained in one of several ways. The incoming letter may be (1) routed by the mail room to the filing department, which attaches the filed material to the letter and then forwards both to the writer; or (2) sent directly to the writer, who decides if he needs the file covering previous correspondence and, if so, requests it from the filing department. In some cases, both the writer and the file are located in the same area, so that the writer can himself secure any filed material he needs.

3. *Permit correspondent to analyze facts and to organize the writing.* To a considerable degree, every letter is an effort to have the recipient believe and act toward a subject as the writer does. Hence, the writer should try to visualize the type of reader to whom he is writing and select an approach that will invoke the reader's response to action. Sometimes, this necessitates guessing or taking a chance. The opening statement, for example, should be designed to get the reader's attention. Following this, the reader's interest should be developed. Then, lead this interest into a desire and finally culminate the entire letter with action—to order the service, to accept the adjustment, to pay the bill, or whatever the case might be. For reports, a simple statement of what the report is about, what it shows, and how the information should be used are of major interest.

4. *Provide correspondent with a stenographer or a dictating machine when ready to dictate.* The assignment of stenographic help to a writer is done by the stenographic supervisor or by the office manager. For corresponding, the stenographer should report to the correspondent at stated times throughout the day; this permits better organization and execution of work on the part of both the stenographer and the correspondent. In actual practice, however, the task of regulating stenographic work is not so simple. Most offices have a certain amount of irregular correspondence which is best handled by adapting it to a schedule setting definite hours when emergency dictation can be handled.

This helps accomplish all the work with a minimum of confusion. On the other hand, emergency work can be sandwiched in with the regular work. However, when this is done, allowance must be made in the regular schedules.

Many report writers prefer to write out the material in longhand before having it typed. Others put most of their material directly on the machine. The type of material, difficulty of composing, and the amount of statistical tables help determine which procedure to follow.

5. *Get material typed.* The final step is the actual physical work of typing the material, and this is by no means a small job. When completed, the material is sent to the correspondent, who reads, checks, and, in the case of correspondence, signs the letters. Subsequently, the material is prepared for mailing or distributing.

TYPEWRITERS

Machine selection is a part of planning. In the work of correspondence and report writing, the typewriter is a basic office machine, is widely used, and speeds the handling of all written work. It should be noted, however, that in this day and age many reports are prepared by computers.

A convenient classification of office typewriters is (1) standard and (2) electric. The former is actuated by hand or human energy, i.e., by the depression of a key. While typing, the carriage is moved to the left by action of a spring. In contrast, the electric typewriter is motivated mainly by electricity. Manual energy is still used to touch the keys, but the energy input is about one-fifth of that required for manual machines. Work done on an electric typewriter is of uniform type impression, and a greater number of copies can be obtained without any increase in manual energy. An electric machine costs more and has fewer moving parts than a standard machine.

Most typewriters on the market today are excellent machines and have many common features which are recognized as standard equipment. Most are equipped with the "set" and "clear" tabulators, either of a single- or decimal-key type. Tabulators are very helpful for the rapid movement and alignment of the carriage which is required in reports and other written work that have frequent indentations. Typewriter platens are available in different degrees of hardness. A soft platen should be used where the number of copies are few and quietness is desired. Conversely, a hard platen is recommended when a large number of copies is required. It causes more noise, however, than does the soft platen.

Figure 9 shows a "Selectric" typewriter which is electric and features the innovation of changing selective typing elements, thus making it

Courtesy: International Business Machine Corp., New York

FIG. 9. An IBM "Selectric" typewriter. This is an electric machine adaptable for various "balls of type" supplying various type styles in keeping with different writing demands. The ball of type or selectric element can be quickly interchanged with other elements. A wide variety of elements are offered.

possible to use the style of type best fitted for the particular writing application. Regular correspondence can be a distinctive type, invoicing of a type that is large, and personal notes of a script style. In general, most typewriters manufactured today are equipped with a standard keyboard. Special keyboards or parts of keyboards, such as engineering, mathematical, chemical, or foreign language signs and marks, are available at an additional cost.

AUTOMATIC TYPING MACHINES

The automatic typing machine has won wide adoption for the typing of similar letters when they are in (1) large quantities and (2) similar format having slight changes only. It consists of a regular typewriter to which a special mechanism has been attached. The paper is inserted in the machine in the same manner as in a regular typewriter; and the date, name, and address are typed in by hand. At the touch of a button, the machine takes over and automatically types the letter, stopping at the first place where a special fill-in is required. This is typed in by hand, and then, after another touch of the button, the machine continues typing the letter to the next stop. Figure 10 shows a letter typed in this manner. All paragraphing, spacing, and the like are handled by the machine. If possible, the location of each fill-in should be at the end of a line or paragraph, to provide the required elasticity in space. Words or numbers of varying lengths can be inserted without difficulty. The entire letter has

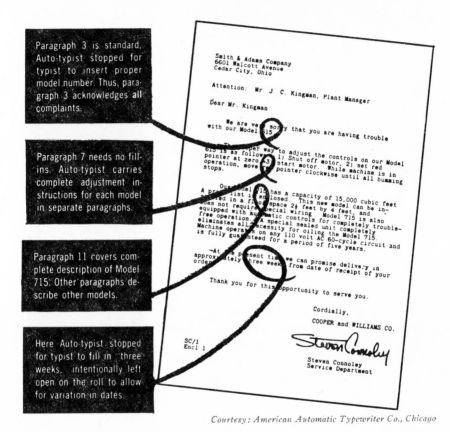

Courtesy: American Automatic Typewriter Co., Chicago

FIG. 10.   A letter typed by an automatic typewriter. Paragraph selection and individual fill-in material are easily handled as described in the illustration.

been typed automatically by machine, with the exception of the individualized parts as noted on the illustration.

As many as 200 short letters a day can be typed with this machine. Multiple combinations of machines, requiring one operator, can produce approximately 500 short letters a day. Such a battery is a mass producer, flexible, and efficient. For most applications, an operator can employ a battery of four automatic typing machines.

Courtesy: *American Automatic Typewriter Co., Chicago*

FIG. 11.   An automatic typewriter featuring push-button controls.

Form letters or paragraphs are originally cut on either (1) a record roll or (2) a tape. This perforating work is done in the individual office or at the local service office. The record roll, resembling that used on a player piano, is mounted in the machine and, when released, passes over a trucker bar in which a vacuum is maintained. Any opening in the roll causes a change in pressure, which actuates the type, thus causing the machine to write. The capacities and details of operation vary with the machine and the manufacturer. Various automatic features, capacities of machines, and special attachments are available. About 20 different letters or an equivalent of form paragraphs can be placed on one record roll. The operator selects the material to be machine-typed by means of simple controls. In one method, a series of push buttons is used to make the operation entirely automatic. See Figure 11.

When a perforated tape is used, the operation of the automatic typewriter is quite similar to that described above. Such a typewriter unit is illustrated in Figure 12. The holes in the tape cause the mechanism to operate specific typewriter keys which result in the desired letter. Perforated tape is being used more and more to operate office machines automatically. The tapes are stored and reused as desired.

Courtesy: *Commercial Controls Corp., Rochester, N.Y.*

FIG. 12.   An automatic writing machine that is actuated by a punched tape.

PRODUCING LETTERS BY DUPLICATION PROCESS

To produce a substantial quantity of written material exactly alike, any one of several duplicating means described in Chapter 5 is satisfactory. Duplicating is fast and economical. It is used for both letters and reports. When used for letters, the name and address are omitted, and simply "Dear Sir" is put on each letterhead, with the name and address on the envelope only. As an alternative, the name and address can be typed

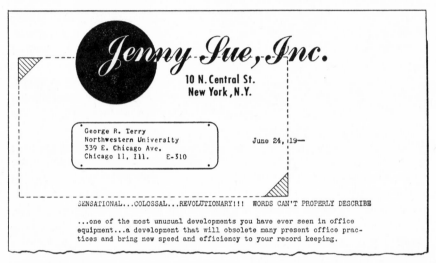

FIG. 13. A "window letter" which features the use of a preaddressed card to individualize a form letter. The card, also used as a business reply card, is held in place either by a pocket in the back or by slots into which opposite card corners are inserted (as illustrated). The name and address appear through a window opening in the letter. The mailing can also utilize window envelopes.

carefully on the letter, but it will not match precisely the duplicated part of the letter. However, with typing skill and experience, satisfactory results are possible.

Another possibility for volume mailings is to use a "window letter." A preaddressed card is attached to the back and top of the duplicated letter, so that the name and address appear at the normal location and can be read through a window opening in the letterhead. The card also serves as a business reply card with necessary postage and name and address of the sender on the reverse side. This arrangement is illustrated in Figure 13.

For correspondence, a machine is available that will write a complete letter from blank paper in one run—individual name and address, salutation, letterhead in color, date, text, and facsimile ink signature—all with one operator. Since the same basic process is used at the same time, the name and address are perfectly matched with the text of the letter. In addition, the machine will print and personally identify a reply card. Sheets of paper are fed automatically to the machine, which progressively prints name, address, salutation, letterhead, date, body of letter, closing, and signature. The machine speed is 100 complete letters per minute.

Duplicating is used in another way in connection with correspondence. This is the growing practice of handwriting a short reply in the margin or at the bottom of an incoming letter. Then, by means of a duplicating machine, a copy is made of the letter and reply. The original and the written reply are sent to the interested party, the copy being retained for the files. The term, "dupli-correspondence," can be used to identify this use of duplicating and is illustrated by the upper portion of Figure 14. While this procedure is not suited for all correspondence it does provide the sender with complete information (his letter and the reply) in a single compact form, seems to be acceptable for many routine matters, and saves considerable typing and filing space. Actually the receiver's filing space is reduced by 50 percent. Under the conventional arrangement the sender mails his original to the receiver and retains a copy. The receiver retains the original sender's copy, writes his reply to the sender and retains a copy of his answer which is filed along with the original sender's copy. The sender files the reply received along with his copy of the originating letter. This is shown graphically in the lower portion of Figure 14.

WHICH BASIS—PERSONAL OR MACHINE?

Either a personal or a machine basis can be followed in writing letters and reports. Under the personal basis, the dictator talks to a stenographer, who manually takes down the statements in shorthand. Later, these notes are transcribed. When the machine basis is used, the dictation is recorded on a machine and subsequently played back to the transcriber, who types the letter.

Advocates of the personal basis are quick to point out that a feeling of close cooperation, better understanding of the type of letter to be written, and consideration for the important human element are induced when letters are dictated to a stenographer. Second, the personal basis permits the transcriber to work from written notes, which are usually easier to comprehend than audible data. Third, with diligent and reasonable effort, shorthand can be mastered. Fourth, the cost of a machine is avoided, as well as the costs of operation, special supplies, and maintenance. Fifth,

ORIGINAL LETTER

ORIGINAL LETTER
WITH ANSWER

DUPLICATE OF
ORIGINAL LETTER
WITH ANSWER

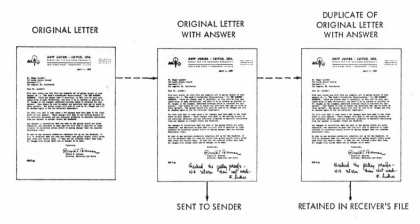

SENT TO SENDER

RETAINED IN RECEIVER'S FILE

SENDER
COPY NO.1 TO RECEIVER
COPY NO. 2 TO SENDER'S FILE

RECEIVER
COPY NO. 1 RECEIVED

FILE

FILE

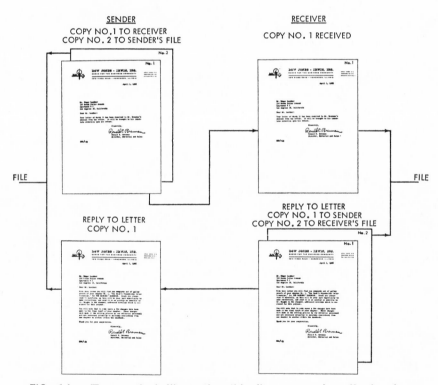

REPLY TO LETTER
COPY NO. 1

REPLY TO LETTER
COPY NO. 1 TO SENDER
COPY NO. 2 TO RECEIVER'S FILE

FIG. 14.   (Top portion) Illustrating "dupli-correspondence" whereby answer to letter is written at bottom of incoming letter and returned to sender; (bottom portion) the traditional practice of mailing original of letter and retaining copy in file.

dictation is possible anywhere. A special machine need not be available. However, a machine for recording dictation can be used. The notes are printed in letters on a tape in accordance with a special code. The machine looks like a small typewriter and requires special training for proficient operation.

The important advantages of the dictating machine basis include the following: First, dictation is expedited—material can be dictated when it is on the dictator's mind. His thoughts can be recorded as they occur to him. Second, the distribution of work among transcribers can be balanced. Steady and even work throughout the day frequently minimizes the number of transcribers needed. Third, the transcriber's time is saved, since her presence is not required while the dictation is being recorded. Fourth, convenience is provided. The dictator can work independently; he can dictate at his convenience; he need not wait for his stenographer. Fifth, the dictator is alone; thus, concentration and clearer and better thinking are encouraged.

DICTATING MACHINES

A dictating machine consists of a recorder unit used by the dictator, and a transcriber unit used by the typist to play back the recorded dictation; or a combination unit featuring both recording and transcribing. The latter is practical when the dictator and transcriber can plan their day for separate periods of dictation and transcription.

The recorder is equipped with either (1) hand microphone, recommended for ordinary dictating practices or when the surroundings are somewhat noisy; or (2) desk microphone, for recording over-the-desk conference discussions or important telephone conversations, assuming the consent of both parties has been obtained. Furthermore, when the recorder is equipped with a foot-control device, the desk microphone permits free use of both hands during correspondence dictation. It is possible to start and stop the recorder as desired and to listen to what has been dictated. A signaling device is also provided whereby the amount of dictation and places of correction can be indicated. There is usually a backspacer for repeating dictation and voice-control adjustments to regulate speed, volume, and tone.

Most dictating machines use a recording medium of either (1) plastic belt, (2) plastic disk, or (3) wax cylinder. One plastic belt medium is an endless belt of thin, tough plastic, $3\frac{1}{2}$ inches wide and 12 inches in circumference. It withstands rough handling, accommodates about 15 minutes of dictation, and serves as a permanent, one-time recording medium. As many as five belts, nested one within the other, will fit into a small business envelope and can be mailed for a few cents. Figure 15 shows a dictating machine using a plastic belt.

The plastic disk is also a satisfactory medium. The disk can be used once, then thrown away or filed for future reference. One hundred disks are approximately 1 inch in thickness; and three sizes are available—3, 5, and 7 inches in diameter, respectively—for 4, 15, and 30 minutes of recording. The disks are light, tough, and unbreakable, which makes it possible to send them conveniently through the mail. Wax cylinders are also in use, but they are used with older equipment. Cylinders are shaved

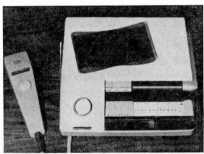

Courtesy: Dictaphone Corp., New York

FIG. 15. Taking up less space than a letter and weighing about eight pounds, this fully automatic dictating machine is a recorder-transcriber unit and employs a plastic belt as the medium.

after usage to remove the engraved surface so that the cylinder can be used again for dictation. A wax cylinder will record about eight one-page letters and can be shaved about 65 times.

BUSINESS WRITING AND MANAGEMENT ORGANIZING

In the office letter writing is done by different employees located in many different departments. Many top executives prefer to handle their correspondence work in their own unit, i.e., by their secretaries and themselves. However, the bulk of correspondence work is usually performed by correspondents who either have transcribers permanently located in the various departments performing letter writing or have transcribers in a centralized transcribing department or "pool."

Whatever the organizational arrangement, the producing of letters requires coordination among various personnel. For example, the dictator must correct or redictate if the transcriber's work is in error, the dictator cannot be effective if the file clerk supplies the wrong materials, and the transcriber cannot be efficient if the dictator does his work poorly. The organizational relationship should foster the needed cooperation and coordination among those engaged in letter-writing work.

Likewise, many employees have the task of report writing. In some cases, the total job content is report writing; in others, a report is required but once a week or month. Report writing can be found in almost any organizational unit—it is not confined to "the office." For example, the assistant sales manager may have the responsibility of writing the monthly sales report; the technician, a research report; and the personnel manager, a report on the company's industrial relations.

MOTIVATING WRITERS OF CORRESPONDENCE AND REPORTS

Many office writers will seek to improve their efforts on their own. This is commendable, but success in this undertaking requires top management support and encouragement. The chief executives must show by their actions that they are interested in better writing by their office personnel and they must initiate and take steps to demonstrate this belief. Casual comments are insufficient, a definite program is needed. Such a formal effort may take many different forms.

An expert's individual criticism of an employee's writing can be highly beneficial. A sampling of the writer's work is submitted to the expert who marks the copies showing how to improve them. Words and phrases are crossed out, stronger words substituted, and punctuation improved. A note explaining the changes is returned with the copies. Most employees appreciate constructive suggestions, but comments about a person's writing must be tactful for no one enjoys being told he writes badly. It is also best to keep the comments confidential for a person will cooperate more readily when he knows the evaluation of his writing is not being made known to his superior.

Supplementing these personal evaluations with private interviews or holding small conferences limited to about five writers are effective. Distributing handout materials showing examples of effective office writing is also recommended. Such literature helps to establish effective writing standards, a favorable attitude toward writing, and specific writing suggestions for certain situations.

A program which acquaints all correspondence personnel with effective letter-writing fundamentals, enumerates specific practices preferred by the enterprise, and supplies the best writing tools will help tremendously in attaining effective letter writing. For example, Mutual of New York undertook a comprehensive correspondence simplification program and, among other things, drafted a series of "guide letters" for its correspondents. Figure 16 shows an example. These letters were meticulously

Example of The "Long" and "Short" of It

DEATH CLAIM - EXPLAINING AGE ADJUSTMENT
Original

We are enclosing a letter addressed to the payee under the above numbered policy, explaining the adjustment which we made because of a difference in the Insured's age.

Will you see that we are furnished with the best evidence available as to the correct date of birth? A copy made by a notary of a family or public record, made at or near the time of birth, of the date of birth together with a statement by the notary as to the date of publication of the book from which the record is obtained, and by whom the record was made and when, is the most satisfactory evidence. Form 3593 covers such information. If no such record is obtainable, an affidavit to that effect should be furnished together with the best information available with a full statement as to its source and why it is believed to be correct.

Please forward the above information to us at your earliest convenience.

Yours very truly,

Revised
To Manager

DCA-14   We will gladly make adjustments on this claim, if necessary, when correct birthdate is established. If (name) is unable to complete Form 3593, please get an affidavit stating why the date is believed correct and return with the best evidence available.

Also, kindly give the enclosed letter* of explanation.

Thank you.

* Key No. DCA-15

Original 160 Words: Revised 53 Words: Saving 67 Per cent

Note: The Original is a splendid example of a letter that goes to great unnecessary length in stating the obvious. Notice that the Revised states all that a manager need be told to know how to proceed.

Courtesy: Mutual of New York

FIG. 16. A guide letter furnished company correspondents to assist them in writing more effectively.

prepared to give customers the answers they wanted in understandable terms and in a friendly, helpful manner.

It frequently is helpful to appoint a correspondence counselor. He or she may be selected from among present employees, or the services of a consultant may be used. The duties of the counselor include those of an adviser, a teacher, and a salesman for effective writing within the enterprise. He is the nominal head of the program for correspondence improvement.

The belief is spreading that typically a writer has only two or three writing weaknesses, not all of them. Intensive corrective work to remedy these few faults, not discussing over and over again all the defects of his writing with him, is the real road to improvement. Further, one learns to write by writing. Active participation is paramount. Listening to suggestions and rules is helpful but indirect, and will never of itself improve the mediocre writer.

Films and other visual means are also popular. They provide a change of pace and afford excellent reemphasis of certain principles and practices. Some excellent films are available.

Some advocate a self-instructional or programmed method by which the subject is taught in many small steps with questioning and answering at each step. The student studies at a pace comfortable for him and advances in the material only after demonstrating mastery of the material already presented. The trainee is required to reply to the questions asked by writing words, sentences, and paragraphs on his answer sheets. He then checks his answers against those given in the material to see how well he has done.

Whatever form of training is followed, there should be periodic checks on the effectiveness of this work. Probably the superior means is to compare samples of the trainee's writing before the instruction work to his writing after completion of selected segments of the instructional program. Such a comparison reveals whether the writer *is applying* what he has been taught to do. It is common practice to have the participant fill out a questionnaire form to give his reaction to the program. Usually such forms are filled out at the middle and at the last sessions of the training meetings. Some claim very satisfactory results from grading each trainee on selected factors and requiring a certain level of attainment based on these scores for employment as a writer. Figure 17 shows such an evaluation sheet.

But don't expect writing proficiency to be acquired overnight. Some learn more quickly than others. The genuinely interested employee and the new employee usually learn more quickly than the long-time employee. It takes time to change writing style and habits. Persistency and continuity of purpose pay off. Commonly a period of between one and two years is required to achieve marked writing improvement.

Each correspondence employee should be kept busy at the level of skill for which he or she is hired. Stenographers should not be tied down to typists' jobs. Correspondents should not spend a great deal of their time filing. High-salaried executives should not dictate letters in those cases where a correspondent will do an equally effective job. Full utilization of all correspondence facilities is the goal. In addition, the machines must be kept in good repair to insure high volume and quality of work.

The same motivating techniques can be used for writers of reports. But in this area, it is extremely helpful to establish the importance of report

Derby Company					
Writer's Evaluation Sheet					

Employee Name _____   Date _____

Department _____   Scored by _____

Conciseness, Completeness, and Emphasis	Points Check Appropriate Blank				
1. Is his writing compact?	4	8	12	16	20
2. Are specific and familiar words used?	1	2	3	4	5
3. Are active present-tense verbs employed?	1	2	3	4	5
4. Is the meaning definite and precise?	2	4	6	8	10
Organization of Material					
5. Is his writing easy to follow?	2	4	6	8	10
6. Do the key points and conclusion stand out?	2	4	6	8	10
Tone					
7. Is his writing friendly and written in a natural style?	4	8	12	16	20
8. Is the "your" viewpoint utilized?	2	4	6	8	10
9. Are courtesy words included?	1	2	3	4	5
10. Does he show understanding of the reader's problems?	1	2	3	4	5
TOTAL					

FIG. 17.   An evaluation sheet for on-the-job office writers.

writing. This will add prestige to the writer as a doer of work that is needed and is beneficial to all members of the enterprise. More specifically, it should be pointed out to the writer how report writing will help him, that reports can be a means to desirable ends—to get certain actions started and others curtailed. The reading of good reports is also helpful. A study of expressions, choice of words, and organization of material can be especially beneficial. Regular meetings to encourage the exchange of ideas helpful to writers are another effective medium. Also, writers should be told to draft their material currently—while it is on their minds. Make a brief written note when you think of an idea which you can use in your writing. Ideas come when least expected and are easily forgotten unless noted.

BETTER DICTATING AND TYPING PRACTICES

The dictator should follow these simple suggestions: (1) have complete information at hand and organize his thoughts before dictating, (2) refrain from unnecessary interruptions, (3) speak clearly, pronounce each word correctly, and avoid the "ah" and "oh" when thinking about the next sentence, (4) be concise—avoid unnecessary details and repetition, and (5) relate complete working instructions—number of copies, general makeup of material, and whether rough draft or final copy is desired.

Proper instructions, adequate supervision, and regular practice are essential for attaining typing proficiency. The office manager should do everything possible to promote these essentials. In addition, he should provide a good working area, including adequate space, good lighting, a posture chair, a desk or stand which insures a comfortable work arrangement, and supplies within easy reach.

CONTROLLING LETTER AND REPORT WRITING

Unnecessary letters and reports are a tremendous waste of time, money, and energy. The office manager should see to it that only necessary materials are prepared and that they fulfill a vital need.

In the typical enterprise too many letters are written. A number serve no genuine purpose and others are replies to communications which do not require an answer. The habit of writing reports tends to remain long after the original need for the report has ceased. Periodic revaluation of the necessity for all reports should be followed. In the case of operative reports, all that is needed is the statement that activities are proceeding according to plans or that they are within acceptable limits. This latter can be called a "tolerance report." If plans are not being fulfilled, the recipient wants to know what is out of line and how best to correct it. Such a report can be termed an "exception report" and is in keeping with the constraint of "practice exception reporting" stated in the previous chapter.

To gain some idea of the extensiveness of writing work, the following simple investigation can be made. Determine the payroll for one month for employees engaged in letter and report writing. Add to this the monthly investment in machines, space, and supplies. View this total in relation to the number of letters and reports written. Compare it also to total office expense. In most cases it represents a sizable percentage.

Answers to these questions aid in attaining better controlling:

1. Is this written material really necessary?
2. Does this written material satisfy the purpose for which it is intended?
3. To whom are copies sent? Should they be sent?
4. Can one copy serve several present recipients?
5. Can the readability be improved by illustrations, better English and grammar?
6. Is the best means being used to produce the written material?
7. Is it worth the cost?
8. Should it be automated?

When given sufficient thought and properly applied, the answers to these questions will assist in writing better—not bigger—letters and reports. And office managers will have achieved a noteworthy accomplishment.

The distribution of reports merits special attention. Too often distribution is made to a long list which includes names of persons who neither need nor read the report. Many practices reputed to be truthful are cited in office management circles regarding efforts to screen the distribution of reports. One such practice is to review the distribution list and remove the names of certain individuals believed nonessential as report receivers. No notice is given those whose names are removed. Subsequently, in most instances, the absence of the report is not noticed by the new nonreceiver; seldom is a complaint or an inquiry made about the report.

It may be argued that the additional cost of running off extra copies of a report is relatively small; that is, to make 24 copies costs little more than to make 14 copies. But while the cost of labor, paper, and machine time for the differential 10 copies may be relatively small, the fact still remains that 10 more people receive the report. They take time to look it over, become interested in functions or problems which may not be their concern, waste some of their time on these "foreign" activities, and require additional filing space and help to retain the reports for some doubtful future reference.

Additional specific suggestions include the adoption of better correspondence and report writing standards designed to attain improved quality and quicker service. Also, some measurement of quality and of output should be determined, for only by such means will a manager be able to determine the success of efforts toward improving the work of writing. Consideration for accuracy, clearness, conciseness, completeness, and naturalness can be used to rate the quality of the work. Output might best be determined by sorting letters according to type and counting the number of each type written during the period of a week or two weeks. For reports, number of pages, by type, usually gives satisfactory results.

An accounting of such things as the machine assigned to each correspondent, the amount of work turned out by each machine, the extent of machine idleness, and the amount and frequency of repairs can also be employed. These data, plus proper follow-up, will help to improve the work output. Desirable in certain instances is the drawing of a daily record or chart for each stenographer or typist, showing the amount of work completed, the amount currently being handled, and the amount scheduled to be done. This information can be used to distribute the work evenly among all employees and to check accomplishment with task.

The use of an office manual is another effective means of controlling. Manuals provide the employee with standard practices and instructions in a form that is convenient and easy to use. They help the employee to help himself and assist in eliminating many needless errors.[1]

COST OF LETTERS AND REPORTS

Cost is among the best approaches for controlling the writing of letters and reports. Few realize what it costs to write a letter or a report. Figure 18 shows an estimate of time and cost factors in writing a typical one-

	Personal Basis	*Machine Basis*	*Form Letter*
Planning the letter	13 min.	13 min.	0 min.
Dictating the letter	13 "	8 "	0 "
Transcribing and typing	7 "	9 "	3 "
Checking and signing	3 "	3 "	2 "
Total Time	36 min.	33 min.	5 min.
Labor cost @ $2.50/hr	$1.50	$1.38	$0.21
Supplies and office overhead	0.50	0.50	0.07
Total Cost	$2.00	$1.88	$0.28

FIG. 18. Estimate of time and cost to write a one-page letter (original and three carbon copies).

page letter. Observe that for the personal basis the cost per letter is $2. Even a form letter costs 28 cents. The cost varies, of course, depending on the length, difficulty of material, method of transcription, and nonproductive time.

The cost for large quantities of almost identical letters can be reduced considerably by using the automatic typewriter. One operator with four machines will produce approximately 500 one-page letters a day. For this volume, using a five-year depreciation basis for four machines and direct labor cost of $20 a day, the cost figures about 6 cents a letter.

Likewise, the cost for identical letters produced by a duplicating process is less than for those individually typed, the exact figure depending mainly upon the process used and the quantity involved. Of course, costs for a letter individually typed and those for a duplicated letter are not strictly comparable, since it is unlikely that quantities of identical letters would be individually typed.

Dept. ______ Report ______
Date ______

PLEASE NOTE

Dear __________:

The cost of preparing this report for you is $ _____. Is it worth this much to you?

We wish to eliminate, simplify, or combine reports which "cost more than they are worth."

Will you let us have your comments on the following lines?

____
____
____
____
____
____
____
____
____
____

Return to Neal Graham
Office Manager

Sign your name here ______________
Your title ______________
Department ______________

FIG. 19. Suggested form to be attached to all reports to make receiver cost-conscious and to eliminate unnecessary report work.

Some office managers have informed the recipient of a report what it costs to prepare it and have indicated that in the future his unit or department will be charged for this work. A simple form such as that shown by Figure 19 is effective in making the recipient more cost-conscious of report preparation. If the costs do not justify the use made of the reports, the recipient will usually request his name to be withdrawn from the distribution list. Discretion and judgment must be exercised in this approach, but it is effective.

The cost of a report depends upon many factors. Expense of gathering data and the time of the writer are key costs. Studies show that what appears to be a simple 20-page report may cost upward of $1,500 to prepare. Most executives underestimate what a report costs. Computer-prepared reports also usually mean a considerable expenditure.

CHAPTER THREE

OFFICE COMMUNICATING

SERVICES

*In about the same degree as you are helpful,*
you will be happy.
—Karl Reiland

SUCCESS in any enterprise depends in great measure upon the ability to communicate effectively and this, in turn, is conditioned by proper use of communicative devices. The various communicative services in an enterprise, such as the telephone and personal messenger service, must be operated in an efficient manner for sustained high office productivity to exist. There are no substitutes for these office services. They must be provided if the office work is to be accomplished effectively.

SELECTING THE COMMUNICATIVE MEANS

Typically, a business enterprise has a variety of communicative means available to it. These include such means as telephone, teletypewriter, intercommunication systems, messenger service (either personal or mechanical), television, and a host of others which will be discussed in this chapter. Mail is also an important means, but discussion of it is delayed until the following chapter. Before the proper means can be selected, it is necessary to know what the real communicative needs of the company are. Various considerations enter into the picture. Without this knowledge, a hodgepodge, overlapping, and noncoordinated communicative system that is not tailored to serve best the requirements of the company is likely to develop. Among the major considerations are:

1. *The quantity and type of communications that should be provided.* This information, segregated for supervisors, salesmen, customers, ven-

43

dors, and the general public, will provide helpful, factual, and basic data.

2. *The cost of the communication.* An approximate cost range from the minimum to the maximum, and related to the service provided, is helpful.

3. *The importance of speed.* Certain devices transmit messages in a matter of seconds, others require several days. Adequate planning reduces much of the need for speed in communicative devices.

4. *Are written or oral communications needed?* The former tend to be more specific, provide evidence, and help to lessen misunderstandings. In contrast, oral communications are quicker, cost less, and are superior when an exchange of ideas to reach a mutual agreement is desired.

5. *The length of the communication.* Certain devices are ideal for lengthy communications, while others are designed for short, terse messages.

6. *The effect of peak load periods.* Volumes vary and the capacity of the selected communicative means must satisfy the peak load.

To gain a quick comparison of various communicative means, Figure 20 has been included. This indicates differences for basic considerations among the several means.

TELEPHONE

Good telephone practices aid in building the good will of any enterprise, save time and energy, and help get work accomplished. The telephone has come into wide usage because it provides an inexpensive, convenient, and rapid means of communication. Referring again to Figure 20, telephone communication is verbal and is not well suited to convey information concerning drawings, sketches, or dimensions of parts. Conversing over the

					COMMUNICATION MEANS			
Is Communication	*Mail*	*Tele-phone*	*Tele-type-writer*	*Tele-graph*	*Tel-auto-graph*	*TV*	*Inter-com*	*Per-sonal Mes-senger*
An oral message?	No	Yes	No	No	No	No	Yes	Yes
A written message?	Yes	No	Yes	Yes	Yes	No	No	Yes
Operative when nonattended?	Yes	No	No	Yes	No	No	No	Yes
Suitable for handling illustrations and drawings?	Yes	No	No	Yes (Wire-fax)	Yes	Yes	No	Yes

FIG. 20. Comparison of common communicative means on basic service factors.

telephone places the participants in a peculiar relationship. The persons talking can hear but cannot see each other. The impression must rely entirely on the voice—its tone, clearness, and pleasantness; the selection of words; and the manner of speaking. All of these factors, properly blended, constitute the art of telephoning, which can be acquired.

Telephone systems can be classified into three types: (1) the outside telephone with extensions handled through a company switchboard (PBX), (2) the private internal telephone (PAX), and (3) Centrex telephone service. The first provides service for external calls coming into or going out of the office and for internal calls between telephones within

Courtesy: Illinois Bell Telephone Co., Chicago

FIG. 21. The new Dial PBX provides an easy, part-time job for the attendant.

the office. However, by using the Dial PBX, outbound calls are dialed directly from every desk, so the telephone attendant can handle incoming calls and perform other work. Figure 21 shows a Dial PBX. In the second type, private internal telephone (PAX), "inside" calls do not go through the switchboard. Since, in the typical company, more than one-half of the telephoning is internal—between telephones within the company—use of the private internal exchange relieves the regular telephone lines. This clears the way for better service on "outside" calls—those from customers and other important callers. The third type, or Centrex telephone service, features Direct Inward Dialing (DID), that is, all incoming calls, local or long distance, can go directly to the extension, which carries its own number—the usual seven-digit number. Centrex needs no switchboard attendants to handle most calls, insures maximum privacy on every call, saves about one-half minute on each call by dialing directly, and provides itemized telephone billing by individual telephone station. Interoffice calls are handled simply by dialing the last four digits assigned to the extension that is called.

The advantages of Centrex service are impressive and numerous successful installations exist. However, adequate survey and study should always be conducted before installing this service. To date, the chief shortcoming is inability to transfer calls automatically. The help of a console attendant is required to transfer incoming local or long distance calls from one extension to another. Also the incoming caller must have the correct number for company, department, and unit; knowing the company's number only is insufficient for direct dialing. Technical requirements sometimes call for equipment installed on premises owned or leased by the telephone company at a higher rate. In general each potential installation should be carefully reviewed and adequate attention given total cost estimates with reference to the service to be provided.

EFFECTIVE TELEPHONING

Certain characteristics distinguish the seasoned and efficient telephone user. We will comment on a few of these characteristics, first, for the switchboard operator and, second, for the individual using a telephone. For each, there are both technical aspects and speech aspects.

Under switchboard operator, technical aspects include the best way to handle the levers, the manipulation of the cords, the dialing of numbers, and the writing of messages, each of which constitutes an important segment of switchboard telephone efficiency. In addition, correct routing of calls is paramount. The operator must know her setup thoroughly and follow a set procedure for handling unusual requests and other types of time-consuming calls. The best way of performing all these tasks can be found by consulting the telephone company's special representative.

Speech aspects include the proper use of the voice over the telephone, the manner of speaking, and the standardization of certain phrases and words in conversation. Proper practices in these aspects help to obtain faster service, better cooperation, and company good will. It may be well to secure the help of a trained consultant in this field. The following expressions are effective:

1. Identify the company immediately. To illustrate, say:

   "Good morning. American Manufacturing Company," or
   "American Manufacturing."

2. If the party must be delayed, the operator should say:

"The line is busy right now. Will you wait?"

3. When the caller agrees to wait, the operator should report about every 30 seconds, saying:

"The line is still busy."

When able to complete the call, the operator should say:

"I'll connect you now. Thanks for waiting," or "Here's the line now. Thanks for waiting."

When the caller cannot wait, his name and number should be obtained and the call returned.

The good work of a private switchboard operator must be supplemented by proper telephone techniques on the part of the individual using the telephone. Helpful suggestions of a technical nature include:

1. To be heard clearly, speak directly into the transmitter, with the lips about 1 to 2 inches from the mouthpiece.

2. To hear better in a noisy office, place your hand over the mouthpiece, not over your ear.

3. To attract the operator's attention, move the receiver hook up and down slowly and evenly.

4. Be prepared to take messages or handle inquiries promptly.

5. After finishing a conversation, replace the receiver gently making certain it is all the way down, otherwise the line is either "out of order" or "busy" to anyone calling.

Speech aspects by the individual user emphasize the following:

1. Answer the telephone immediately and identify the department and yourself. For example, say:

"Cost Department, Mr. Allen."

If answering for someone else, give his name and then yours. Say:

"Mr. Brown's office. Miss Kenny speaking."

2. Handle, if possible, but transfer the call when it requires handling by someone else in the company. To do this, advise the calling party he is being transferred to another phone. Say:

"I will transfer you to our accounting division. One moment, please."

Then flash and tell the switchboard operator:

"This call to Mr. Kohl."

3. When using the telephone, do not leave the line unless it is necessary. If this is the case, tell why and for how long. Say:

"Will you excuse me for a moment? I must look at our file on this."

4. On outgoing calls, introduce yourself promptly. Say:

"Hello, Mr. Briggs. This is Spencer of National Sales."

Periodic checkups on the use of the telephone by company personnel are in order. All calls should be handled in the prescribed manner. Data can be obtained on the time required to handle calls and on the manner of speech. Concentrate on the promptness in answering the telephone, helpfulness on all calls, and a pleasing telephone personality. Employees should be informed that periodic checkups are made. When necessary, remedial action should be taken without delay.

INCREASING TELEPHONE EFFICIENCY

In too many offices adequate attention is not given to telephone usage; waste is allowed to creep in, costs rise, and the telephone service and customer relations are not what they should be. Proper telephone efficiency is not maintained by any one easy method such as circulating a memo to the effect that telephone waste must stop. For satisfactory results, a more sophisticated plan and mode of operation are required. Study should be made to determine the facts and from them to identify *in general* the major causes of the waste. With such a background, the corrective actions to take can be intelligently formulated.

Among the common causes are:

1. *Incoming calls are poorly routed and handled.* A call is transferred several times before the proper party is reached. No established means for handling out-of-the-ordinary requests are followed. Callers are asked to "hold the line" for unreasonable periods.

2. *Excessive personal and unnecessary outgoing calls are made.* Certain employees are spending more time telephoning than their job requirements suggest. Telephones are busy most of the time in office units whose work does not entail contact with the public. Call-backs must be made to obtain information that was not requested on the first call or because initial call was poorly planned—data not readily available, called party not in, or requested information already in possession of party calling.

3. *Employees interrupted due to telephone.* These interruptions are costly; they can occur either while performing other duties or while

telephoning. The former breaks a work or thought pattern, the latter delays completion of the telephone call, ties up the line that much longer, and commonly annoys the other party to the telephone call.

4. *Employees do not have enough work to do.* The conditions of lack of urgency about completing assigned tasks, too many employees and insufficient work volume can easily lead to excessive telephoning, especially of personal calls. Telephoning can be a convenient fill-in to give the appearance of being busy. For many office jobs it is a part of the work, but its essentiality should be determined.

5. *Telephone facilities are not suited to requirements of present office.* This happens in stable as well as in growing offices. New telephone facilities are constantly being offered. In light of these developments, current facilities become obsolete and should be modified or exchanged to improve telephone efficiency.

In any specific case where these or other malpractices are known to exist a remedial plan of action can be initiated and vigorously launched. Note again the statement above "to identify *in general* the major causes of the waste." Too much valuable time can be wasted in trying to pinpoint specific telephone culprits, in attacking symptoms rather than causes. Where evidence is found that employees don't have enough work to do, the solution is simple. Adjust workforce and make certain that supervisors are scheduling sufficient work to each employee and following up to assure that work is finished promptly. Adjustment can be by transferring employees, attrition, scheduling vacations, changing work, or even laying off. In many many instances of telephone waste it will be found that correcting the lack of sufficient work is the remedy.

In addition, to the extent that it is practical, establishing schedules for telephoning in and out of the company is effective. This can reduce interruptions, spread the telephone load by placing outgoing calls into periods when incoming calls are light, and tends to concentrate outgoing calls—all factors that make for better telephone usage and efficiency. Furthermore, request your telephone company to review your equipment. Supply their representatives with the information you have obtained regarding present telephone usage. They will be glad to recommend and show what additional equipment, if any, is needed, how to eliminate obsolete units and modernize your telephone facilities to meet current needs.

Also, a program involving employee participation is usually effective. Telephoning is almost a universal activity by office personnel and their efforts in improving telephone efficiency can be sensational. All office personnel—department heads, supervisors, and nonmanagers—should be a part of the program. Specific opportunities for the reducing of current telephone waste should be shared and the reasons for the program explained. Such opportunities stem from data on common causes listed above. To these, employees should be encouraged to add their own suggestions. From all this a definite target should evolve, thus supplying a needed goal against which efforts can be evaluated. While the program is in progress, employees should be kept informed of accomplishments and interest maintained in the program. The end-results should be well publicized and favorable recognition extended for the accomplishments achieved.

AUXILIARY TELEPHONE SERVICE

It is possible for several executives in different parts of the country to hold a conference by means of a simultaneous telephone hookup known as *conference call service.* The savings in time and trouble from this type of service are obvious. In some instances, the connections are monitored or recorded for possible future reference. When this is done, approval by the parties is necessary. The signal that the call is being recorded is a "beep" tone every 15 seconds.

A perpetual telephone receptionist is afforded by the *automatic answering device.* This unit, about four times the size of a telephone, is linked to the telephone. Incoming calls are answered by a recorded message something like this:

"This is the Avenue Realty Company. Your call is being answered by an automatic answering device. Will you leave your name, telephone number, and message after you hear the 'beep' tone? You may leave a half-minute message for me, and I'll call you when I return. Thank you."

After returning to the office, all messages recorded by the unit are audited and the return calls made. The device is especially convenient not only for small, one-man offices and for medical doctors, but also for large offices during the nonworking hours, thus providing around-the-clock service. The cost is $30 per month after an installation fee of $15.

Radio-telephone service provides communication between moving units and any Bell System telephone. It is particularly adaptable for use by trucking, taxicab, and public service companies, and by police and fire departments. For a two-way communication, a mobile unit is called by means of a regular desk telephone. A request is made for the mobile service operator who, by means of radio, signals the driver of the mobile unit. This is done over an approved radio channel. The driver answers the call on his dashboard telephone, and the conversation takes place. In a similar manner, the driver can call his office from his mobile unit. In contrast, the one-way service signals only to the mobile unit. By means of a code, the driver translates the message, such as "Go to Warehouse R immediately."

The *teletypewriter*, or TWX service of the telephone company, provides some 60,000 subscribers with a two-way teleprinter transmission. Speed averages about 75 words a minute. The machine used resembles a large typewriter that transmits messages between stations using telephone lines. Basically the keyboard of the machine is standard and when the keys are depressed, electric impulses reproduce the message in typed form on one machine or on many similar machines, the number being determined by the number of connections desired. To send a message, the TWX subscribers' directory is consulted, the call is placed by number, and the connection is made. Any two

teletypewriters can be connected for communication in the same way as two telephones. The communication is two way; a written conversation can be carried out. The service is especially effective over long distances. Charges are made on the basis of time and distance, similar to the long-distance telephone. Rates are approximately two-thirds to one-half those of the telephone. Figure 22 shows a teletypewriter.

Additional services include:

WATS, or wide-area telephone service. This provides unlimited interstate telephoning within specific areas for a flat monthly rate. Such a service is designed for the

Courtesy: Illinois Bell Telephone Co., Chicago

FIG. 22. A teletypewriter.

customer who makes frequent calls to widely scattered and distant points.

Leased Private Lines. These insure availability of the circuit for the customer who is provided exclusive use between two or more locations for a scheduled period each day. This service is preferred when a large volume is sent regularly to a small number of fixed points.

Dataphone. Machines are able to talk to each other by means of this service. It is very important in the transmission of data in the language of a computer. Dataphone is fully discussed later in this chapter.

TELEGRAPH

A well-known means of handling communications over relatively long distances is the telegraph. Telegrams secure attention, provide terse businesslike messages, and impel immediate action. They are used for practically all subjects or phases of business activities.

Telegraphic communications can be sent by any of four main ways: (1) over the counter—giving it to the operator at any branch office; (2) by messenger; (3) by telephone—similar to an ordinary telephone call, charges being made to the telephone account or paid by coins dropped into a public pay telephone; and (4) by mechanical tie lines, such as direct telephone connection which is simply a direct wire between the sender's office and the local telegraph office. There is also a *Telex* service offered by the telegraph company. This includes a teleprinter network so that any Telex subscriber can communicate with any other Telex subscriber. The teleprinter is a machine similar to a typewriter which transmits the typed message electrically to the telegraph office. Transmission is at the rate of 66 words a minute. The message is recorded on paper tape both in the sending office and in the telegraph office. The former serves as the sender's reference copy; the latter is used to transmit the message to a circuit for its destination. Telex subscribers pay special low rates for this service.

The cost of regular telegraphic communications varies with length of message, distance, and speed of delivery. Domestic messages are classified into the following main types: full-rate telegram—most expedient service; base rate applies to 15 words; (2) day letter—deferred slightly in handling; base rate applies to 50 words or less and is roughly 40 percent more than that for a full-rate, 15-word telegram; (3) serial—a deferred message sent in sections to the same addressee during the day; cost is about 20 percent more than for a day letter containing the same number of words; and (4) night letter—an inexpensive overnight service; base rate applies to 50 words or less and is about 75 percent of that of a full-rate, 15-word telegram.

Cablegrams or services to foreign countries are classified as (1) ordinary—the standard full-rate service, (2) urgent—priority over all other messages except government messages, (3) deferred—no priority over other types, and (4) night letter—messages permitting overnight delivery.

Code words are sometimes used for telegraphic communications in order to reduce costs or to insure secrecy. For example, the code word "ROEUZ" might mean: "What action shall I take?" Commercial codes are available, or a special code can be created.

Anything printed or drawn, such as layouts, drawings, or charts, can now be transmitted instantly and accurately by WIREFAX, a special service using telegraph equipment. Actually, WIREFAX is a public facsimile system that transmits in units up to $7\frac{1}{2}$ by $9\frac{1}{2}$ inches. Cost depends upon amount and distance. Charges for the initial unit between Chicago and New York are about $5, and each additional unit is about 50 cents.

There are also machines supplying the transmission of printed documents, drawings, and charts. Coaxial cable, private microwave system, or the facilities of common carrier services can be used. The selection depends upon volume, speed, and distance involved. Figure 23 shows the unit that converts document images to video transmission signals. Another unit returns these signals to the document images. The quality of the copy is excellent.

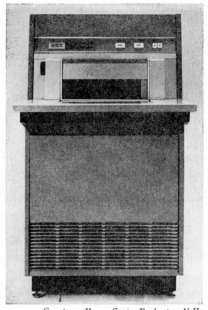

Courtesy: Xerox Corp., Rochester, N.Y.

FIG. 23. This unit transmits written, typed, or printed documents at high speeds, either within a building or across a continent.

TELAUTOGRAPH

Another well-known means for transmitting messages is the telautograph. As the name suggests, it transmits a handwritten message. The writing is electrically reproduced mainly, but not exclusively, over comparatively short distances. It is popular for communication between main office and receiving room, department and department, and warehouse and main office. In order to send a message, a switch is turned on, and the message is written with a metal stylus on a metal platen. To see what is being written, the sender watches the pen of the instrument writing on a roll of paper. Figure 24 illustrates a telautograph. As the message is written, it is reproduced almost simultaneously at one or a number of connected points.

A telautograph provides economical and high-speed transmitting and receiving of messages. Handwritten records are furnished and can be attached to such things as inquiries, notices, and shipping instructions. It is possible to carry on a written conversation—messages can be sent and received.

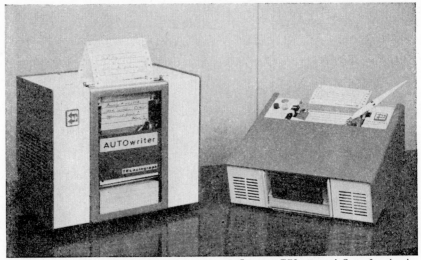

Courtesy: TELautograph Corp., Los Angeles

FIG. 24. TELautograph receiver and transmitter instruments which handle handwritten messages, including special symbols and sketches.

CLOSED-CIRCUIT TELEVISION

One of the newer methods for transmitting messages is television. Although its current application in business is limited, television holds much promise for the future. By means of closed circuits, it is possible to transmit and have instantaneous receipt at many points. Television presents the message visually and in motion—a series of events. However, it does not provide a written message to the recipient.

An interesting application concerns railroad freight car reporting wherein cars move by a TV camera stationed at a strategic point in the freight yard. Pertinent data are viewed on the side of the car and transmitted to a policing and recording center. Floodlights provide proper illumination for both day and night operation.

A television-telephone, enabling the caller to see as well as hear the party at the other end of the line, is available. When the caller lifts the television-telephone, his image appears simultaneously on one-half of his screen and upon one-half of that of the party being called. When the party answers, his image appears on the remaining halves of the two screens. The unit is about the size of a conventional television table model set. Maximum effective distance is several miles. Television-telephone applications include those in large industrial plants to compare drawings and materials, in banks to check signatures, and in penal institutions to serve as an electronic guard.

INTERCOMMUNICATION SYSTEMS

Quick verbal communication is provided by means of intercommunication systems. Within an enterprise the various individuals or stations are commonly each equipped with a speaking-talking unit. By turning a switch or pushing a button, instant right-of-way is obtained with anyone in the circuit, and conversations can be conducted with great clarity of tone. When privacy is desired, the microphone in the unit can be turned off and a handset substituted.

Figure 25 illustrates the chief advantages of using intercommunicative units. All these add up to better service at lower cost. Cases are on record where, by use of an effective intercommunicative system, a company has saved as much as $1,500.00 a year in employee time and reduction of other communicative means. Figure 26 provides a format to determine the cost of handling verbal communications within an office. In the illustration an expenditure of $7,500 is estimated, an amount which warrants efforts to see that these communications are handled in the best way.

Many different capacities and features in units are available; usually, it is advisable to consult with the manufacturer or sales representative for specific data regarding individual requirements. The units can be connected in various circuit arrangements, depending upon the needs of the particular enterprise. Figure 27 shows models of intercommunication units.

Intercommunication systems are especially effective for communicating *within* an entire enterprise. Locations for the units could include areas of not only the office, but also engineering, production, warehousing, and shipping. This "all-to-all" communication is well illustrated by Figure 28. Observe that some units are speaker units only, the need for talking units in some locations being unnecessary.

PAGING SYSTEMS

Important in most companies is the means of locating people through the use of flashing lights, tone bells, and buzzers. These paging devices are usually run by the telephone switchboard operator, or they may be a part of a private internal telephone system or of the intercommunication system. The light or noise outlets are located throughout the office and plant, so that key personnel are free to leave their desks without fear of

Get the answers right away. Talk instantly to the individual you want. Your channel to him is always open. Even if he's on the phone when you signal, you alert him without breaking in on the conversation. And with Executone's paging facility, you'll contact him anywhere on the premises.

More efficient customer service. Because Executone frees phone lines for outside calls, customers reach you more easily. And you can check their orders or get information for them over your Executone without ending your phone conversation!

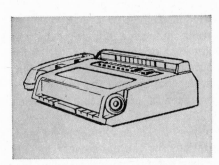

Eliminate extra phone charges. With telephone intercom you pay rent every month for every phone, hold button, and intercom light . . . and for each relay unit that this equipment requires. Your rugged, dependable Executone system— which you own outright—ends all this. You save on your phone bill every month!

Free your phones for outside calls. Inside calls need an inside channel of communication, separate from your telephones. Keep your phones open for important outside calls. Don't make customers wait . . . or call back. They might decide to call someone else!

Courtesy: Executone, Inc. Long Island City, N.Y.

FIG. 25. Advantages of using intercommunicating units.

A. Indicate the number of intercommunicative facilities in your office, factory, laboratories, and other buildings.............................   20
B. About how many internal calls per station per day are made? (If unknown, tally such calls for a week or so.)....................................   5
C. The total of internal calls per day is..............................   100
    (A multiplied by B)
D. Estimated time in minutes for an internal call......................3 minutes
E. Expressed in hours, and realizing there are two people in each conversation, the time for internal calls per day is......................... 10 hours
    (Multiply C by 2 by D and divide by 60)
F. The average hourly pay per conversant is...........................$ 3.00
G. Daily cost for internal calls is therefore...........................$ 30.00
    (E multiplied by F)
H. Based on 250 working days per year, the annual cost for internal calls is therefore...$7,500.00
    (G multiplied by 250)

FIG. 26.   Determining the cost of handling verbal internal communications.

missing any calls. By means of a code, such as two long and two short rings for the president, one long and one short ring for the controller, and so on, these men are notified of calls. By calling either the switchboard operator or a designated person, the message is obtained. The system is quite effective, for it is convenient and is a time-saver to all concerned. The latest paging units feature soft sounds in quiet areas and adequately loud sounds in noisy areas.

Courtesy: Executone, Inc., New York   *Courtesy: Scan-Am Co., McHenry, Ill.*

FIG. 27.   Intercommunication units enable the user to converse with any other master station or any staff station in the system. The communication is extremely fast and clear.

INTERNAL DISTRIBUTION SERVICE

In the normal course of office work, many papers are handled within the enterprise successively by several employees. As already noted, mail is distributed, notices and memorandums must be delivered, and reports must be sent to executives. All these activities necessitate adequate

ALL-TO-ALL COMMUNICATION

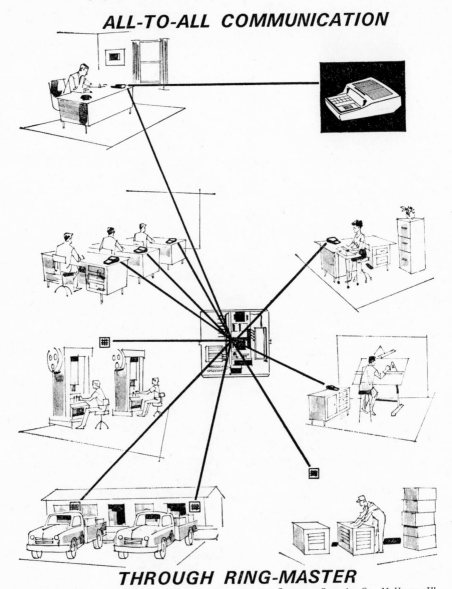

THROUGH RING-MASTER

Courtesy: Scan-Am Co., McHenry, Ill.

FIG. 28.   Intercommunicating units provide "all-to-all" communication.

distribution facilities. Either a personal or a mechanical means can be followed. Selection depends upon the specific objectives, but usually the following are of prime concern:

1. The total number of papers and messages.
2. The frequency of the papers and messages.
3. The number of delivery points.
4. The number of papers and messages at each delivery point.
5. The distance between delivery points.
6. The maximum allowable time between delivery points.
7. The expense, including investment and operating costs.
8. The flexibility of the service to meet changing office conditions.

PERSONAL MEANS FOR CARRYING MESSAGES

The personal method is the oldest and the most common means for distributing papers and messages. To be of greatest benefit, the service must be regular and frequent. Schedules should call for deliveries about every half hour throughout the office. This time interval can be varied, depending upon the needs. In some cases, calls every 15 minutes might be required; in others, calls every hour might suffice. Very often, calls are made with greater frequency in the early morning and late afternoon business hours, in order to take care of the peak loads.

Deliveries can be made either on a desk-to-desk or on a departmental basis. The former is preferable and should be used whenever possible. Desk-to-desk calls insure that the person intended to receive the material actually gets it, that messengers do all the messenger work, and that the distribution and collection are accomplished with a minimum of effort and confusion. In contrast, deliveries by departments require further distribution within each department and often result in costly delays.

The personal method for carrying messages provides excellent training for new, inexperienced employees. They can quickly learn the names of key employees, location of their work stations, layout of the office and plant, and the work of each organizational unit. Some large companies start all young office help as messengers before transferring them to their initially selected jobs.

Adequate control of the messenger service requires close supervision and adherence to these practices:

1. The complete route must be established to include all desks designated as stations. The course to be followed must be defined, and the allowable time for one trip must be known. Adequate rest periods between

trips are desirable and usually amount to about 20 percent of the total travel time.

2. All desks designated as stations must be visited on each trip. Even though there is nothing to deliver, there might be something to pick up.

3. Messengers should confine their efforts to the delivery and pickup of written materials along the prescribed routes. The running of miscellaneous errands for members of the office should be forbidden.

4. Each member should be instructed to sort the papers as they are collected, so that on each trip, deliveries can be made to stations not yet called upon. Papers designated for stations already called upon are delivered on the next trip. This eliminates backtracking.

5. A designated area or receptacle for "incoming" and another for "outgoing" messages should be used at each station desk.

6. Each messenger should be provided with an accordion file with one section for each station or some similar arrangement. The file should be equipped with a shoulder strap for carrying, or mounted on wheels for pushing, from station to station.

7. A card-control system provides a check upon the activities of messengers. Several plans are possible.

a) The messengers can be required to check in, that is, to sign or punch a card at several well-selected stations along the route. These cards can be collected daily and inspected, and any irregularity of service can be investigated and corrected immediately.

b) The messengers can pick up a card and replace it with another at each station on the route. Different cards, identified by number or color, can be used for each trip; and by noting the card in the basket, spot checks can be made to find out if schedules are being maintained.

8. To inform employees politely of the last trip for the day, the messenger can either say, "Good night," or leave a card printed "Last collection has been made" in the basket.

MECHANICAL MEANS FOR CONVEYING MESSAGES

Mechanical conveyors are well suited to convey papers and messages when the work volume is large and fairly constant, and where stations remain fixed. Belt conveyors are probably the most common type used in an office. Brush-off stops can be provided at each station in order to permit the delivery of papers at specific points. Figure 29 illustrates a conveyor belt being used to transport orders within a stock brokerage office.

Pneumatic tubes are effective, easy to use, and do not require special skill to operate. Material is carried quickly and accurately to its destination. The initial cost of the tubes is rather high, but the maintenance cost is low. The use of pneumatic tubes is most economical where the volume of work is large. Different-sized tubes and tube carriers are offered. For example, a "4-inch tube carrier" is a popular size and has maximum inside length of 14 inches. Rectangular-shaped carriers are also available for handling bulky items. In the case of a large aircraft manufacturer, the installation of pneumatic tubes linking seven buildings into one unit resulted in annual payroll savings of over $100,000. For a medium-sized metal processor, messenger service costs were cut $4,200 a year by use of pneumatic tubes.

Courtesy: Merrill Lynch, Pierce, Fenner, and Smith, Inc., New York

FIG. 29.   Effective use of conveyor to transmit papers in an office.

AUTOMATED DATA AND THEIR TRANSMISSION

Many of the communication means already discussed are used for transmitting data of a nonautomated classification, that is, the data are not in or out of a computer, nor are they a part of a source data automated arrangement whereby office machines are tied together as a unit, with the source data being automated. The progress of automated data processing, either by computer or a source data arrangement and, especially, where there is a central physical location of a major portion of the data processing, has emphasized the need for efficient transmission of large volumes of data. The result is that a host of data transmitting machines have been perfected and are now available on the market.

To illustrate, a centralized accounting operation necessitates that information be consolidated from sources located over a widespread area. This arrangement is shown by Figure 30. Data can be sent to the computer headquarters by mail, messenger service, telegraph, or telephone. For any of these communication means, the data can be sent in computer language, but telegraph or telephone provides much faster service. Telegraph has been used extensively and is efficient, but developments now tie the ordinary telephone to a computer and provide multiple and direct access to it. The development making this possible is called Data-Phone; the machine utilized is illustrated by Figure 31.

FIG. 30.   Centralized accounting arrangement requiring data from widespread locations.

Regular telephone lines comprising a nationwide network are used, and there are no intermediate steps. To utilize the Data-Phone, a customer picks up the telephone and dials the service number. A dial tone signals connection, after which he inserts an identification card into the device attached to the telephone, which identification is required by the computer and confirms the customer's right to order. Then the data, in the language of the computer—punched cards, perforated tape, or magnetic tape—are fed into the device; and these data are transmitted at speeds up to 1,600 words a minute directly into the computer. Machines talk to one another, cross-town or cross-country. Payment for each Data-Phone call is made just like a telephone call and at the same rate. Its potential is believed to be so great that in the not too distant future, conversations between machines over regular telephone lines may exceed the volume of voice communications.

An economical way to handle a flow of communication is by means of a machine shown in Figure 32. To transmit data, the operator either types

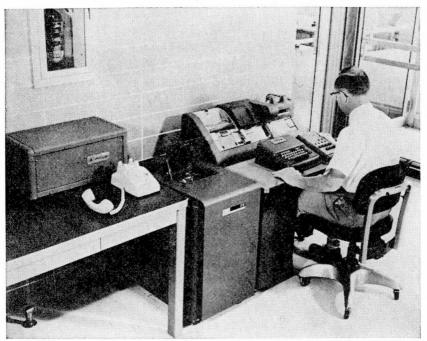

Courtesy: Illinois Bell Telephone Co., Chicago

FIG. 31. The units to the left constitute Data-Phone. To the right, punched cards are being prepared.

the message or feeds a perforated paper tape of the message into the machine. As this is done, the communication is printed in identical form on another similar unit or units in the same building, or city, or thousands of miles away. The distant machine follows every move the operator makes; when three lines are skipped, the receiving unit skips three lines. The machine illustrated is a send-receive set, meaning it can send and receive data. These machines are being used for sending and receiving bank checks, invoices, personnel records, and ordinary messages. By this communicative means, permanent and accurate records on standard business forms are provided both sender and receiver, thus minimizing misunderstandings and errors. When the input data are typed, the machine will supply a perforated tape of it, if desired. Such a tape can be used for reference or for transmitting the same data again at some future date.

In addition, communication machines are now available that transmit duplicates of documents or records for several yards or for thousands of miles. To operate, the original document—like a letter, list of quotations, or invoice—is inserted into the machine. Almost simultaneously, an exact

Courtesy: Teletype Corporation, Skokie, Ill.

FIG. 32. A modern and versatile machine for data communication systems used for direct communication with data processing equipment.

duplicate of the document is produced at the receiving machine. Actually it is a long-distance duplicating machine. There is no conversion of the data into perforated paper or magnetic tape, that is, into machine language. All data are in a familiar form—printed, typewritten, or handwritten.

RECEPTION SERVICE

To many visitors, the first impression of a company is frequently gained from the receptionist. Courteous and prompt treatment should be extended visitors in order to build and develop company public relations and good will. The receptionist's basic job is to (1) find out with which person, if any, the visitor should talk; and (2) arrange for the visitor to see the proper person quickly.

A pleasant manner of speech and a winning personality are highly important; but in addition, certain standardized practices have been found most effective. For example, in securing information from callers, the receptionist should ask: "What company do you represent?" or "May I help you?" Should the visitor say he is calling about a personal matter, or words to that effect, it is well for the receptionist to inquire: "Does Mr. —— know you?" If an evasive or a negative reply is given, the receptionist should ask if someone has sent the caller. If no one has, a recommended statement is: "I'll let you talk with Mr. ——'s secretary, who will try to help you."

When the person called on is too busy to see the caller, the receptionist should address the visitor with: "I'm sorry, Mr. —— is busy and will not be able to see you. Can you come back or telephone first for an appointment?" In situations where the person is absolutely not interested in talking with the caller, the receptionist must be tactful and courteous. Refusals to grant short interviews with callers should be held at an absolute minimum; but when necessary, the receptionist might say: "I am sorry, but Mr. —— is not interested in what you have to offer." Under no circumstance should the receptionist suggest that the visitor call later if the person being called upon has no intention of seeing him. Honesty is the best policy.

The receptionist must be fully familiar with what matters are handled by each employee who has callers. Normally, a guide or booklet is available for reference. Customarily, the receptionist keeps a report of callers, including the date, the name of each caller, the name of his company, and the person called on. When individual conditions permit, the receptionist might also perform office work of sorting, stuffing envelopes, typing, or operating the telephone switchboard. However, if there is too much extra work, the regular duties of the receptionist might be neglected. The office manager should watch this carefully.

TAPE AND WIRE RECORDERS

These devices are being put to a large number of uses, including the recording of inventory counts, personnel interviews, laboratory tests, and sales talks. In the case of inventory counts, the person taking the count is equipped with a microphone attached to the recorder in the office. As the inventory count is obtained, it is spoken and thus recorded. A typist then

Courtesy: *Webster-Chicago Corp., Chicago*

FIG. 33.   A high-fidelity recording and playback tape recorder.

plays the recording and types the inventory lists. Intermediate paper work, tally sheets, and the like are eliminated. Likewise, interviews with prospective employees or, in the case of lawyers, talks with clients can be recorded and studied for complete information—a more effective practice than the use of handwritten notes, which often inhibit the speaker. However, when conversations are recorded, approval by both parties is normally necessary. Tape or wire is used in the operation of the machine. The tape is a narrow, thin, flexible, paperlike material coated on one side with magnetic oxide of iron; when wire is used, it is of a special type. A recorder is slightly larger and heavier than a portable typewriter. Figure 33 shows a popular tape recorder.

CHAPTER FOUR

THE OFFICE MAIL

The easiest thing of all is to deceive one's self;
for what a man wishes he generally believes to be true.
—Demosthenes

IT IS doubtful that a modern enterprise could exist without mail; it is imperative that some written means of offering the services of the enterprise, answering inquiries, and issuing statements and invoices be available. The office mail constitutes an important facet of office services. When handled efficiently the entire office is aided. However, if handled haphazardly, as evidenced by inconveniencing and costly errors, the service of the office is hampered. Since handling office mail is the lifeblood of an enterprise, it merits careful attention.

THE KEY CONSIDERATIONS

Promptness and accuracy are the major requisites of satisfactory mail service. From the managerial viewpoint of the individual enterprise, there are four key rules to follow faithfully: (1) keep mail addresses and routes up to date, (2) use efficient means for sorting, delivering, and picking up mail, (3) mechanize wherever volume is sufficient, and (4) know and apply proper postage rates.

KEEP MAIL ADDRESSES AND ROUTES UP TO DATE

One of the greatest steps forward in mail addressing is the Zip Code. This is a five-digit code designed to expedite and economize mail handling, by quickly identifying destination area, and to facilitate optical reading equipment to be used by many large U.S. post offices. The first digit designates one of ten national service areas. The second digit identifies the service subdivision, the third digit the post office in that subdivision, the last two digits the post office station from which the mail to that addressee is delivered. Figure 34 shows the Zip Code National Areas along with authorized two-letter state abbreviations. Using these abbreviations will enable city, state, and Zip Code to be written on one line by most addressing machines. Note that Colorado is CO, Connecticut is CT, Illinois is IL, and Texas is TX. National Code Area No. 6 includes

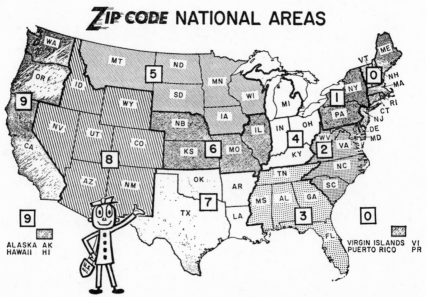

Courtesy: Post Office Dept., Washington, D.C.

FIG. 34.   The Zip Code national areas and authorized two-letter abbreviations for the various states.

Illinois, Missouri, Kansas, and Nebraska. Figure 35 shows the Zip Code for Illinois. Chicago, for example, is 606; the second digit—zero—identifies the northeast part of Illinois, the third digit—6—identifies the Chicago Post Office. To these three digits is added the local zone number in Chicago. Hence, a Zip Code for an address in Chicago, Illinois, is 60611.

There are nearly 600 major post offices and sectional centers and about 42,000 different Zip Codes. The program starts with mass users of second- and third-class mail. They are required to update their mailing lists to include the full Zip Codes. Beginning January, 1967, all such mailers must presort their mail to the full five-digit Zip Code before mailing. Eventually all business mailers will be included in the complete Zip Code usage.

Answers to selected questions of greatest interest in Zip Code are shown by Figure 36. Review of this illustration provides pertinent information in this interesting subject area.

Courtesy: Post Office Dept., Washington, D.C.

FIG. 35.   Zip Code for subdivisions in state of Illinois.

It should also be observed that the maintenance of a mailing list can best be described as a task of perpetual revision. If the office is small, the names and addresses can be kept in an indexed book. For large offices the list is represented by magnetic tape, by filed punched cards, or addressing plates arranged in a specific sequence. But whatever form is used, no mailing list is permanent. Certain names and addresses must be removed, revisions made on others, and new ones added. It is not uncommon to find 18 to 20 percent of the addresses on a mailing list become obsolete within each twelve-month period. Updating the list, therefore, is a major chore, but a necessary one if the potential effectiveness of the listing is to be maintained.

SORTING, DELIVERING, AND PICKING UP MAIL

Proper arrangement of the equipment in the mail room will help keep the mail moving in and out of the office without interruption or confusion. The work of the mail room can be greatly simplified and performed quickly and smoothly by using the proper number of units, correctly arranged.

Figure 37 suggests a layout for a modern mail room. The equipment has been arranged in a room with dimensions of 12 × 16 feet. Beginning at the lower right of the figure, the route of incoming mail is first to the table where the mail is opened and the time stamped, then to the adjacent tables and sorting racks, where it is sorted. It is then delivered to the proper stations throughout the office.

---

1. Does every patron of the postal service have a Zip Code number?

No. Delivery areas, not mail patrons, are identified by the code. Up to 5,000 offices and homes are included in some Zip Code areas.

2. Who benefits by the use of Zip Code?

Everybody in and served by the postal service. The post office benefits because service is expedited and the user benefits because he receives better service.

3. Will you be more specific? How does the post office benefit from Zip Code?

By reducing the time to process mail, eliminating unnecessary handling, and increasing the efficiency of the service. Zip Code determines destinations and not so much time will be spent on reading addresses and sorting mail. Personnel can devote more of its time to handling the mail more expeditiously and with greater accuracy. Further, Zip Code will facilitate the transition to optical scanning equipment whereby machines will read the Zip Code numbers and sort mail automatically.

4. How about the large volume mailer, what are his benefits?

He can use his electronic automated equipment to arrange his mailing lists in sequence according to the Zip Code. Further, he can sort his mailings by the code to its destination points. Receipt of the bundled and pouched mail by the originating post office will enable such mail to be sent directly to the transportation terminal for immediate dispatch to the Sectional Center or post office of destination. In many cases this prepared mail will eliminate five or six mail handling steps and improve delivery time by 24 hours or more. For nationwide, heavy-density mailing, sorting by the five digits of Zip Code is practical. For nationwide, light-density mailing, sorting to the first three digits is suggested, and for mailing of a local nature, sorting only to the last three digits is recommended.

5. How can the large volume mailer make the transition to Zip Code without incurring prohibitive cost?

Cost is incurred in adding the code to addresses, but it need not be prohibitive and does represent improvements and better service in the future. To the large volume mailer, the post office provides either a deck of punched cards or a magnetic tape to suit the type of equipment used. These cards or tape contain a master file of Zip Codes for all points in the United States. Also made available is a generalized computer program adaptable to the equipment of the large mailer. By feeding the master file into the computer of the large mailer, addresses are matched with appropriate Zip Code.

6. What about the large mailer without a computer?

The post office will provide a master file of Zip Codes so that the Zip Code can be stamped into the addressing plates or added to the file of addresses.

7. Are there any restrictions on the space requirements of the address?

Yes, only official abbreviations are to be used and a maximum of a 23-position line is designated, made up as follows: 13 positions for the city, 1 position between the city and state designation, 2 positions for the state designation, 2 positions between state designation and Zip number, and 5 positions for Zip Code. Each address must contain a Zip Code. If the "city-state-Zip number" line capacity of a mailer's equipment is less than 23 positions, he should consult his local postmaster for help in the necessary conversion procedures.

FIG. 36. Answers to common questions about Zip Code.

Outgoing mail is first taken to the outgoing-mail sorting racks and tables, shown at the upper left of the figure, where it is grouped with other mail having the same destination. When necessary, each piece is weighed and proper postage determined; then, it is put through the metered-mail machine and finally into the mailbag located at the upper right portion of the figure. Mail is delivered to the post office in these bags.

Weight is also an important consideration in determining proper postage. A mail room should be equipped with an accurate postal scale. Many different models are offered on the market.

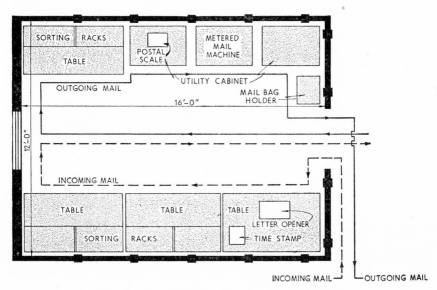

FIG. 37.　Arrangement of mail-room equipment.

The work of handling *incoming mail* consists of fairly well defined and uniform steps including:

1. *Receiving and opening the mail.* Mail is delivered to the office either by the postman or a company representative who calls for it at the post office. The latter is preferred by many large enterprises, especially in the case of the first morning mail, because when called for at an early hour, it can be distributed by the time the office formally opens. In this event, employees handling incoming mail should report for work about one-half hour before the regular opening office hour.

Mail is opened either by hand or by machine, depending upon the volume of mail. For manual means a good standard is 15 pieces per minute. Machines will open as many as 500 letters per minute. Mail marked "Personal" or addressed to specific individuals is not company mail and may or may not be opened, whichever is the policy of the company. The common practice is not to open it. In some instances, mail so addressed is forwarded immediately to the employee's home address.

2. *Sorting and time stamping.* The next step is to remove the contents

Courtesy: First National Bank in Dallas

FIG. 38.   Handling the incoming mail in a large bank.

of the envelopes and, at the same time, sort the mail according to who handles the particular type under question; this might be a department, a division, or an individual. Usually, the name of the person or of the department to whom the letter is addressed determines where it is to be delivered. When this is not given, a quick scanning of the paper is necessary to determine its proper destination. In exceptional cases, the entire contents must be read.

Figure 38 shows a portion of a large mail room. The man in the foreground is opening letters by means of a machine. The man in the background is sorting to the proper compartments in the sorting racks. The general pattern of the various compartments in the rack is similar to that of the mail stations in the office, for in this way the sorted mail can be kept in a logical order for ultimate distribution.

In the case of mail containing money or checks, a listing showing the senders' name and address and the amount enclosed is made out by the mailing department. The cash and checks, along with the listing, are later sent to the cashier department. In other instances, the check is attached to the letter; or in the case of cash, the money is placed in a small envelope and attached to the letter, with appropriate notation. The checks and cash are then delivered to the cashier department.

A letter referring to previous correspondence can either be delivered to the department concerned, which, if necessary, requests the file from the filing department; or it can be sent to the filing department, where the needed file is attached and forwarded to the proper correspondent. The method used depends chiefly upon the number of such letters received and the system of filing used.

At the time the mail is read and sorted, it is customary to stamp the hour and date received on each piece of correspondence. This provides a timed receipt that can be used as evidence in controversial matters regarding the correspondence. It can also be used for checking the efficiency of mail distribution in the office. Either a hand stamp or a machine can be used for the stamping.

3. *Distributing the mail.* This is the final step in the handling of incoming mail and is usually done by messengers, although other means, such as conveyor belts and pneumatic tubes, may be utilized.

For *outgoing* mail, the major areas of mail handling are as follows. Normally, the same employees handle both incoming and outgoing mail.

1. *Collecting and grouping by destinations.* To help in collecting, outgoing mail is usually placed in special desk trays specified as mail stations. Upon receipt at the mail room, the mail is first grouped according to geographical area, then by city, and then by name of addressee. Sorting racks are commonly used for this purpose. All mail of a similar class, and addressed to the same wholesaler, branch, or company, is put together so that it can be mailed as a single piece. Frequently, large Manila envelopes with the address printed or stenciled thereon are used for these large firm mailings. In some instances, each of the outgoing sorting racks contains an addressed envelope which is handy for instant use. Replenishments are made either the first thing in the morning or at regular intervals throughout the day.

2. *Inserting, sealing, and stamping.* If necessary, the material is folded and inserted by the mail department. When ordinary envelopes are used, the name and address on the material must be checked with that on the envelope. Sealing and stamping can be done either by hand or by

machine; the volume of mail should determine the method used. It is possible to seal and stamp around 350 letters an hour by hand. It is advisable to appoint one mail-room employee as sole custodian of the stamps. He should control their use either by affixing the postage to the letters or packages personally or by seeing the letters or packages it is going on before issuing postage to someone else.

When manual operations are used, the stamps are usually kept in an "out in the open" manner, and this may result in stamp losses owing to carelessness in handling and borrowing. To minimize these losses, an accounting should be maintained to show the number of letters mailed in comparison with the amount of stamps purchased. Special care must be exercised in the case of packages.

3. *Mailing the material.* It is advisable to post mail at regular intervals throughout the day. This practice smooths out the work load, minimizes the usual late afternoon peak, and helps the post office to deliver mail promptly. On distant mail, this practice might save a day. Also, knowledge of train and plane schedules is helpful in expediting mail. It is necessary to deliver certain classes of mail to the post office.

MECHANIZE WHEREVER VOLUME IS SUFFICIENT

The use of computers has already been mentioned in connection with the preparation of mailing lists with Zip Codes (Figure 36). Automated means for printing the address on a label are common, and mechanical units are available that fold and insert the mailing piece into an envelope, seal it, address, stamp, and sort by Zip Code. There are various other versatile units of mail machines. They are highly efficient, but their application is usually regulated by the volume of mail to be handled. For this reason, mail work in many smaller offices remains primarily manual.

Popular and gaining even greater popularity is the meter-mail machine that imprints the postage seal either directly on a letter or, in the case of a package, on an adhesive paper tape which is affixed to the package. At the same time the postage seal is imprinted, a "meter ad," postmark, and date are also imprinted. This is illustrated by Figure 39. The machines are offered in an array of capacities and designs; many seal as well as stamp the envelope.

An important part of this machine is the meter, which is a detachable, portable unit containing the printing die for the postage and a recording mechanism. In buying postage, the meter is taken to the post office and set for a lump sum which is paid in advance. The set meter is then returned to the place of business and inserted into the machine, from which metered

FIG. 39. Illustrative of metered-mail imprints, showing "meter ad," postmark, date, and amount of postage.

stamps can be printed as and when needed. In essence, *a postage-meter machine is a government-licensed device for affixing postage.* Figure 40 illustrates a postage-meter machine. Meter mail has many advantages, including the following: (1) Time and effort are saved; (2) stamp losses are stopped; (3) accurate accounting of postal expenditures is provided; (4) date of mailing is shown; (5) quicker handling is provided by the

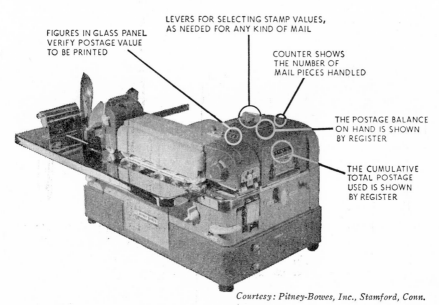

FIG. 40. A postage-meter machine, with the important operations of the meter illustrated.

originating post office, since no canceling is required; (6) the prestige of the user is increased; and (7) postmark, slogan, and advertising are added.

The meter advertising provided by the use of a meter-mail machine offers the advantages of low cost and flexibility. Cost of the printing plates are nominal and easily interchangeable. Then too, simply by turning a dial on the machine the advertisement can be omitted. Meter advertising attracts attention and is virtually isolated from competitive messages. The advertisement itself is of a relatively small size but can be very effective for slogans, reminders, announcements of special events, and the promotion of worthy public causes such as those of supporting charitable groups or preventing forest fires.

Actually, whatever the product, service, or cause meter advertising can normally assist in selling it, but the ad must be given adequate creative thinking and proper timing. Being a supporting medium, it is effective as a part of a working campaign in which it has a definite role to play. This means that the same imprint should not be used over and over again. A schedule of the various prints should be followed to maintain reader interest, employ new appeals, and take advantage of seasonal opportunities as they appear. A number of manufacturers have adopted the practice of supplying the needed plates to their distributors and dealers, thus gaining additional selected readers. Such plates can stress themes such as basic product appeals, new product announcements, and suggestions to tune in on the manufacturer's nationwide weekly TV program.

Certain criteria should be met by meter advertising. The advertisement should be centered around a theme acceptable to a large portion of its potential readers. In brief, it should be in good taste, and not be concerned with political issues or the joining of groups or societies dealing with highly controversial issues. In addition, neither the design nor text of a meter advertisement should suggest any regular postal marks, symbols, or legends. The advertisement should not interfere in any way with the work of the post office.

KNOW AND APPLY PROPER POSTAGE RATES

Key mail personnel must know the postal costs and requirements, so that the proper amounts of postage—no more and no less—are affixed. Knowledge of the various classes of mail is basic. In general, first-class mail includes correspondence, securities, and documents; second-class mail, newspapers, magazines, and other periodicals; third-class mail, unsealed printed matter and form letters; fourth-class mail, packages and parcels. Special services, such as registered mail, certified mail, special delivery, and special handling, are available but should be used only under the right circumstances. Useful information on domestic postal rates and fees is shown by Figure 41 (pages 78–79).

ADDITIONAL SUGGESTIONS

The following suggestions should be adopted:

1. *Include Zip Code in the address.* This speeds delivery. The post office offers assistance in providing Zip Codes. Consultation with authorities of the local post office is recommended.

2. *Use standard-sized envelopes.* Standard-sized envelopes are best suited for most purposes. The No. 9 or No. 10 envelope for correspondence is preferable, since only two horizontal folds in the enclosed material are necessary.

The postage-saver envelope permits third-class rates, yet gives the appearance of first-class mail. Also, the two-in-one combination envelope is recommended where a folder or booklet is sent with a letter. With this type of envelope, the letter or other first-class mail is in one compartment, while the folder or other third-class mail is in another compartment. Illustrations of the postage-saver and the two-in-one envelope are shown in Figure 42.

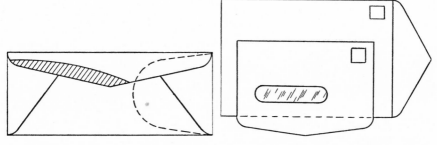

A postage-saver envelope requiring only third-class rate can be top-sealed like a first-class envelope. One end of flap remains unsealed to permit postal inspection.

With the two-in-one combination envelope, first-class mail in one compartment and third-class or fourth-class mail in the other can be mailed as a unit.

FIG. 42.   A postage-saver envelope and a two-in-one combination envelope.

3. *Use window envelopes when feasible to do so.* The risk of getting a letter in the wrong envelope and the necessity of sending individually addressed envelopes to the mail room are eliminated by the use of window envelopes. There is also a saving in cost. With regular envelopes, the labor

SPECIAL SERVICES OF THE POST OFFICE INCLUDE:

1. Special Delivery

This service provides for immediate delivery by the post office serving the one receiving the mail. Special delivery is handled and transported like first-class mail and does not insure safety of delivery or payment of idemnity. For weight not more than two pounds the charges in addition to regular postage are:

First-class and airmail . . . . 30¢

All other classes . . . . 55¢

2. Special Handling

Applies to fourth-class mail only and provides expeditious handling and transporting to the post office serving the one receiving the mail. Parcels sent special handling are delivered same as ordinary fourth-class mail on regular scheduled delivery trips. The charge in addition to regular postage for not over two pounds is 25¢. Higher charges apply for heavier parcels.

3. Registered Mail

All mailable matter sent either first-class or airmail may be registered. This provides added protection for important mail and evidence of mailing and delivery is obtained. The charge, in addition to regular postage, depends upon the declared actual value and whether the mailer has commercial or other insurance. To illustrate, for $5,000 declared value, the charge is $3.00 if such coverage is not in effect.

4. Certified Mail

This service provides for a receipt to the sender and a record of delivery at the office of address. Certified mail is handled as regular first-class mail, no insurance coverage is provided. It is available on any mailable matter of no intrinsic value and on which first-class postage has been paid. The additional fee for certified mail is 30¢, for restricted delivery, 50¢.

5. Return Receipts

Closely associated with certified mail and registered mail, return receipts provides for various types of detailed receipts. Included in the schedule of rates charged are the following:

Requested at time of mailing

Showing to whom and when delivered . . . . 10¢

Showing to whom, when, and address where delivered . . . 35¢

Requested after mailing

Showing to whom and when delivered . . . . 25¢

6. Additional notes

Large bulk mailers should include return instructions in case of post office inability to make delivery. This way obsolete addresses can be removed from their mailing lists. The charge for such returns is nominal. Consult local postmaster for full details and suggestions.

MAIL IS CLASSIFIED ACCORDING TO CLASS, AND THE RATES CHARGED VARY AS TO CLASS, WEIGHT, AND DESTINATION. THERE ARE FOUR MAJOR CLASSES INCLUDING:

1. First Class

This classification includes handwritten and typewritten material. All sealed mail is first-class. Pieces must be at least 3-inches in width (height) or 4¼-inches in length and of a rectangular shape. The rates are:

FIG. 41.   Salient information regarding postal services, fees, and rates.

Letter (surface) . . . . 5¢ per ounce or fraction of an ounce.
Letter (airmail) . . . . 8¢ " " " " " " "
Post card (surface) . . . 4¢ each
Post card (airmail) . . . 6¢ each
Business reply card (surface) 6¢ each
Business reply card (airmail) 8¢ each

2. Second Class

Included are newspapers and periodicals which have been registered with the Postal Department. The sender obtains permission to use this class. Charges vary with distance and weight.

Within county of publication:

Rate per pound . . 1.25¢ Minimum rate per piece . . 0.125¢
Issued more often than weekly (newspaper) . . . . 1¢ per copy
Weighing 2 ounces or less (periodicals) . . . . . . 1¢ per copy

Outside county of publication:

Rates vary for zone and range from 2.8¢ to 14.0¢ per pound

For qualified nonprofit associations such as religious, educational, scientific, and labor groups:

Rate per pound . . . 1.80¢ Minimum rate per piece . . . 0.125¢

Transient—copies mailed by public:

Rate is 4¢ for first 2 ounces; 1¢ for each additional or fractional ounce, or the fourth-class rate whichever is lower.

Controlled circulation publications—contains 24 pages minimum, not over 75 percent advertising, issued at regular intervals of four times or more regularly, and circulated free or nearly so.

Rate per pound . . . 13.5¢ Minimum rate per piece . . . 1.000¢

3. Third Class

Unsealed material not designated second class and having a weight limit up to one pound. Includes circulars, books, catalogues, and other printed matter. Common examples are advertising circulars including printed letters sent in identical terms to several persons.

Single Rate:

4¢ for first 2 ounces, 2¢ for each additional ounce or fraction

Bulk rate:

12¢ per pound, minimum rate per piece, 2.875¢

For authorized nonprofit senders:

6¢ per pound, minimum rate per piece, 1.250¢

4. Fourth Class

Includes merchandise, printed matter and other matter not included in first-, second-, or third-class. The rate varies by weight and destination. Two pounds for a local zone is 29¢, whereas forty pounds for zone 2 (up to 150 miles) is $2.10. Special rates for catalogues and books are granted. The latter is 10¢ per pound and 5¢ for each additional pound or fraction, without regard to zone. Parcels must not exceed 72-inches in length and girth combined. Length is along the longest side and girth is the distance around the thickest part of the parcel.

FIG. 41—Continued.

costs for addressing are about $10 per thousand (assuming a rate of three a minute and wages at $1.80 per hour). Window envelopes cost about $2.50 per thousand more than regular envelopes, so the net saving realized by using window envelopes is $7.50 ($10 less $2.50) per thousand, or 75 percent.

However, some people believe that window envelopes are less attractive and dignified than regular envelopes. Certain types of correspondence are probably best handled by regular envelopes. The final decision in this matter rests with the manager.

4. *Employ enclosed business reply envelopes to increase returns and lower costs.* A permit, for which no fee is paid, must be obtained to use these envelopes. The postage for such envelopes is of a collect-on-delivery type for which the initial sender pays 7 cents for each reply, based on a 5-cent regular charge plus 2 cents for the return privilege. If the return is less than 72 percent of the original mailing, the use of business reply envelopes results in savings. When regular stamped envelopes are enclosed, the postage for 100 replies is $5; postage on 72 business reply envelopes is $5.04.

5. *Have posters, books, and guides available to mail personnel so that they can find out and apply the proper mail procedures.* The *United States Postal Guide* (which can be obtained from the Superintendent of Documents, Washington 20402, D.C.) is especially recommended. The office manager should cultivate close cooperation with officials and employees of his local post office. They are always very helpful and can greatly assist in solving mailing problems.

EVALUATION OF MAIL HANDLING

Mail handling both in and out of the office has been and probably will continue to be a controversial subject of conversation. Mail affects each of us; at times we expect the impossible in mail handling and at other times we are pleasantly surprised with what is accomplished. Commonly, we forget the extent and scope of mail handling. Typically, the office manager wants the mail promptly; he will not even listen to the explanation or reasons for its delay. When one stops to realize that for 5¢ a letter dropped in anyone of a million mail boxes will be delivered to a specified address anywhere in the United States, one can only conclude that the postal system is a fabulous operation and accomplishes much more than the average person is at first prone to acknowledge. And there are many steps required to process a letter. These are shown visually by Figure 43. It requires a lot of manpower, facilities, and management know-how to accomplish this mail work.

THE PICTORIAL STORY OF A LETTER

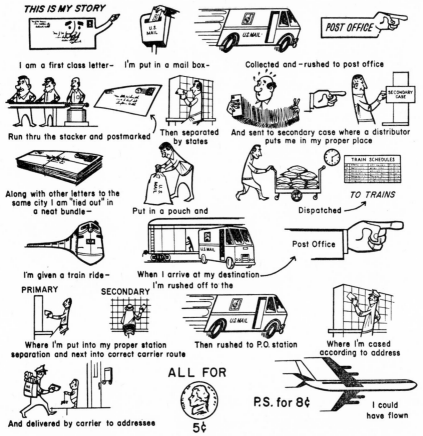

THIS IS MY STORY

I am a first class letter—   I'm put in a mail box—   Collected and—rushed to post office

Run thru the stacker and postmarked   Then separated by states   And sent to secondary case where a distributor puts me in my proper place

Along with other letters to the same city I am "tied out" in a neat bundle—   Put in a pouch and   Dispatched   TO TRAINS

I'm given a train ride—   When I arrive at my destination— I'm rushed off to the   Post Office

PRIMARY   SECONDARY

Where I'm put into my proper station separation and next into correct carrier route   Then rushed to P.O. station   Where I'm cased according to address

And delivered by carrier to addressee   ALL FOR 5¢   P.S. for 8¢   I could have flown

Courtesy: Post Office Department, Washington, D.C.

FIG. 43. Many operations are required to process a letter.

Improvements are being made and more are on the way. The volume of mail is skyrocketing and the demands placed upon the service are increasing. With these changes and excluding technical considerations, several issues emerge as basic. The first is that the postal service is precisely just that—a service. It entails much manpower. While some of the work can and will be automated, a large portion of it cannot. This is an important factor in its rising costs. Manual means are costly. Second, adoption of a simplified rate structure seems to be in order. The present schedules have grown "like Topsy," modifications and changes have been made, but for the most part represent patchwork onto a complicated pattern. A complete overhauling to establish a simple, readily comprehended structure appears highly desirable. Lastly, our philosophy of the postal service requires crystalization. Stated succinctly, is it a service provided by the government such as that of our Department of State, defense efforts, and so forth, or is it a service that should directly pay its own way financially? Perhaps some reasonable compromise between these two views, expressed in measurable terms, represents the needed practical answer.

CHAPTER FIVE

DUPLICATING

Criticism should not be querulous and wasting,
but guiding, instructive and inspiring.
—Ralph Waldo Emerson

DUPLICATING is a basic office operation and is increasing in importance as the work of the office is being modernized. Single copies of papers rarely suffice in the modern office; duplicated copies are needed—in some instances several copies, in other cases thousands. The task is commonly to make or "run off" copies of a report, form letter, bulletin, price list, chart, drawing, or financial statement.

MANAGERIAL CHALLENGE OF DUPLICATING

No office service has undergone more new developments and basic changes during the last several decades than has duplicating. Many new duplicating processes and machines have appeared on the market. This revolutionary expansion of duplicating has brought with it the challenge for adequate management of this office service. Fundamental questions arise. For example, "Are copies really needed?" If so, "What minimum number will suffice?" "Is it better to print computer output on regular forms, or on transparent paper or direct-image master plates for reproduction?" "Should we make or buy most of our office printing needs?"

These are not easy questions to answer; they require sound managerial decisions and actions which are subject to both periodic review and interpretation. Among the basic considerations are:

1. *The quantity, quality, speed, and flexibility of the duplicating service.* What is really required based on reasonable justifications and analysis?

2. *The total investment in duplicating.* This includes not only equipment but personnel and the quantities of paper and supplies held in stock. The cost versus service comparison is also included in this consideration.

3. *The controls utilized.* Duplicating should be scheduled and per-formed within reasonable time and cost limits. It should insure security of classified information, be adjusted to changing needs, and be properly allocated costwise to units for whom the service is provided.

4. *The logical integration of duplicating with related office work.* Does the duplicating simplify and assist in the essential work being done? Is it in keeping with the major goals sought?

DUPLICATING PROCESSES

Basic knowledge of various duplicating processes is helpful in selecting the process to utilize. Figure 44 shows pertinent information on a comparative basis for a number of different duplicating processes. The

Process	Relative Cost of · Duplicated Sheet	Usage	Usually Economical for Number of Copies Up To:	Main Type of Material for which Suited*	Speed in Sheets per Minute
Contact	High	Average	10	T-S-D-P	8
Xerography	High	Average	15	T-S-D-P	6
Stencil	Low	Wide	5,000	T	200
Direct	Medium	Average	300	T	150
Offset	Low	Average	10,000	T-S-D-P	150
Indirect	Medium	Limited	300	T	200
Multigraph	Low	Average	10,000	T	150
Whiteprint	Medium	Limited	500	T-S-D	8
Photocopy	High	Limited	5	T-S-D-P	5
Noncarbon	High	Limited	4	T	5

* CODE   T = Typed or Printed   S = Script   D = Drawing   P = Picture

FIG. 44.   Comparison of various duplicating processes.

contact process, for example, has a relatively high cost per duplicated sheet, enjoys average usage, is usually economical for up to ten copies, is suited for typed or printed material, script, drawings, and pictures, and is produced at the rate of eight copies a minute. Individual requirements should govern the selection and take into account not only the type of data in Figure 44, but also such factors as the cost of the equipment and the supplies to run it, the quality of copy desired, time and place considerations, and employees' preferences.

The various descriptions of these duplicating processes are:

1. *Contact.* This means is rapidly growing in popularity and consists basically of placing a sensitized paper in contact with the material to be reproduced and inserting it into the machine, which exposes, develops, and

fixes the copy sheet. The process is technically known as thermography and means literally a "burning" process. Dark areas, such as typewritten words, absorb more heat than the blank areas. Exposure to infrared light causes the words of the original to burn an image onto the heat-sensitive copy paper. Representative of the contact process is Thermo-Fax and Readyprint. Figure 45 shows a Thermo-Fax copying machine, which makes direct copies in a matter of seconds. Exposure timing is set on the dial on the right of the unit. The original and sensitized papers are placed together and inserted into the machine, which starts automatically and

Courtesy: Minnesota Mining and Manufacturing Co., St. Paul

Courtesy: Eastman Kodak Co., Rochester, N.Y.

FIG. 45. Thermo-Fax Copying Machine featuring speed, economy, and convenience.

FIG. 46. Readyprint Copier for fast, single-copy needs up to 8½ x 14 inches.

makes the copy. It gives ready-to-use, dry copies and emits no detectable odor. The process is effective wherever carbon is present in the writing, as with pencil or typewriter. Readyprint gives exact copies of letters, including original letterhead and signature, and other papers, is always ready to go, produces top quality copies, and is easy to operate. Figure 46 shows a Readyprint Copier.

2. *Xerography* (pronounced zē-rog-ra-fē). This word stems from the two Greek words meaning "dry printing" and is identified as a dry, fast, electrophotographic copying process. Xerography uses light and static electricity to make copies of anything printed, typed, written, or drawn. Copies are made on ordinary paper in a matter of seconds. A specially coated plate is charged with positive-charged electricity and is subsequently exposed to the material to be reproduced, *A*, by means of a camera. As a result, the reflection of *A* on the plate is retained and remains charged positively. The remaining area of the plate loses its charge

because of light exposure permitted by the camera. Then, a negatively charged powder is adhered to the positively charged A. A sheet of paper is placed over the plate and given a positive electric charge. The positively charged paper draws the powder from the plate, forming a direct copy which is heated in a few seconds to fuse the powder into a permanent print. The copies produced are clear, sharp, and permanent. The same plate can be used hundreds of times. The operation is completely automatic. Figure 47 shows the popular Xerox 914 Office Copier. Although not yet

Courtesy: Xerox Corp., Rochester, N.Y.

FIG. 47. The Xerox 914 Office Copier makes perfect copies of all colors as well as rigid three-dimensional objects, in black on white, on ordinary paper or selected paper offset masters.

commercially available, the xerography principle applied to commercial printing is being studied.

3. *Stencil.* This is a common means and consists of "typing a stencil," either by typewriter with ribbon removed or nonoperative, by special hand tools (styli), or by a die-impressed operation performed by the manufacturer. The openings thus made in the stencil, i.e., openings caused by the stencil coating being pushed aside and exposing the base fiber, permit ink to pass through so that paper held against the surface receives the image. Even, sharp, and clear strokes on the stencil give the best results. Corrections can be made on the stencil by using a special fluid to reseal the surface and then retyping. It is also possible to block out and remove an area and replace it by attaching a new portion of stencil. The image or

printing is usually in a jet-black color, although several other colors are also available. It is possible to store the stencil for use at a later time; about 5,000 copies can be made from one stencil. A stencil duplicating machine is shown in Figure 48.

4. *Direct or liquid process.* In this process, the material to be reproduced is put on a master sheet which has behind it a special carbon layer. The carbon places the image in reverse on the back of the master sheet. Different carbons are used for different colors. The master is placed

Courtesy: *A. B. Dick Co., Chicago*

FIG. 48. A duplicating machine using the stencil process.

Courtesy: *Ditto, Inc., Chicago*

FIG. 49. A direct or liquid-process duplicating machine.

in a machine, and copies are made directly from it in this manner: The copy sheet is slightly moistened with a special fluid before contacting the back side of the master; and as the copy sheet presses against the master, a very small layer of the carbon is removed and impressed on the copy sheet. Four colors can be reproduced in a single machine operation, and about 300 copies can be made from one master. Master sheets can be stored for reruns. Figure 49 shows a liquid duplicator.

5. *Offset.* The offset process is subject to many variations. Basically, the principle involved is that the material to be reproduced is (1) prepared on a plate, which is (2) transferred to an intermediate agent, which is (3) printed on the paper. Frequently, the intermediate agent is made of rubber.

One important offset process is photo-offset. The material to be reproduced is photographed, and the negative is transferred to a sensitized plate. This plate is then used in a photo-offset printing unit. Slight variations in this method are commonly termed "planographing" and "offset lithography." Frequently, a xerography process is used for making offset master paper plates.

A well-known process known as "multilith" is based on this offset principle. Either a metal or a paperlike master can be used. The latter is more widely used, since it can be handled like a piece of paper. That is, a regular typewriter plus pencil, pen, ink, brush, or crayon furnished by the supplier are used in preparing the master. Erasures and corrections are handled as with ordinary paper, and the paperlike masters can be filed in the office like paper sheets. The process is recommended for quantities— over 500 and up to 10,000 copies. An illustration of the machine is shown in Figure 50.

6. *Miscellaneous processes.* There are many more duplicating proc-

Courtesy: Addressograph Multigraph Corp., Cleveland

FIG. 50.   A widely used duplicating machine—the Multilith Offset 1850.

esses—too many to include all of them here. In addition to the above, however, mention of several others is warranted. The *indirect* process, also known as the gelatin process, consists of putting the material on a master

Courtesy: Charles Bruning Company, Division of Addressograph Multigraph Corp., Cleveland

FIG. 51. A flexible, high-speed, heavy-volume duplicating machine. Multiple copies of letter-sized originals of small engineering drawings are produced at the rate of over 30 per minute.

sheet made of special paper; the master sheet is pressed against the gelatin, thus depositing the image on it. Copies are then made by pressing the sheets against the image in the gelatin. *Multigraph* employs either an imprinting or a ribbon process of reproducing. In the former, type, rubber strips, or electrotypes are used. The medium is inked and paper coming in contact with the wet type forms the copy. In the latter, or ribbon process, the duplicating is done through a ribbon similar to that used in standard typing, and the finished work closely resembles original typing. The type used is held in a segment or blanket and consists of up to 70 lines of type. Signature attachments are available, changes or corrections can easily be made in the type, and the process is speedy, as up to 9,000 copies can be run in one hour. *Whiteprint* provides a black on white directly from translucent originals. Machines using this process are efficient and produce copies quite economically. See Figure 51 (page 89). Additions to the master is a feature. For example, a customer's statement can be typed on a translucent paper and retained as a permanent copy by the company. At the end of each month, a whiteprint is made of the entire statement and is sent to the customer. Advantages include: No copying work is required, errors are held to a minimum, and each month the customer receives the full story on his account. The process is flexible and can handle large sizes of paper. Either the copy is given a light coating of a special solution to develop the copy permanently or it is exposed to controlled aqua ammonia vapors. *Photocopy* is one of the oldest duplicating processes. By photographing a negative, it is possible to make a positive paper print, that is, black lines with white background. Prints can be made in the same size as, or larger or smaller than, the original. *Noncarbon* utilizes carbonless "NCR paper" of the National Cash Register Company. The bottom side of the first sheet is coated with a colorless chemical and the top side of the second sheet with another chemical. Writing on the first sheet reproduces instantly on the second sheet, and similar reaction takes place between the remaining sheets of the pack. Clear copies are obtained, smears and smudges are eliminated, and hands and clothing are not soiled.

COMPOSITING, COLLATING, AND BINDING

Type compositing, collating, and binding are tasks frequently connected with duplicating work. Type compositing is preparing the type for the master copy. Different styles, sizes, headings, and the like are commonly utilized to make the duplicated material more readable and to highlight important facts. For this work office composing machines are widely used. They bring the versatility of a well-equipped printing shop into the office and are used to prepare type of all sorts for reports, bulletins, booklets, catalogs, price lists, and house organs, where variety in composition is desired.

Figure 52 shows an office composing machine. It resembles a typewriter in both appearance and operation. Each type face is on a removable disk which can be quickly inserted into or removed from the machine.

FIG. 52. Changes from one type to another are accomplished quickly by means of small type fonts weighing less than one-fifth of an ounce. Two such fonts fit into the machine at one time, and changes are made in less time than it takes to refill a mechanical lead pencil.

Each disk is complete with capital and lower-case letters, numerals, and symbols. Over 600 different sizes and styles of type, ranging from 5½-point newspaper style to 14-point Heavy Gothic type, and including boldface headings and italics, are available. Even margins on both the left and the right, similar to those of regular typeset composition, are obtained by typing each line twice. To illustrate: line 1 of the copy is typed in the regular manner on the left half of the piece of paper. Then, it is retyped on the right. The machine spaces the second typing so that both margins are even. The procedure is repeated for each line. When completed, the typed material on the right half of the paper constitutes the finished or master copy.

Collating is the assembling of several different sheets of paper to form a report or booklet. This work can be done manually or by a hand or electrically operated machine. Figure 53 shows collating machines.

In many cases, the material is held together by a binding, of which there are many different types. First, there is side wire stitching, i.e., on the side. Also, there is saddle wire stitching, i.e., through the fold at the back of the booklet. Usually, the latter is preferred, since it enables the sheets to remain flat and open once they are placed in that position. Mechanical fasteners are used extensively, including ring or loose-leaf binders, prong fasteners, or screw-post fasteners. Also the use of wire and of plastic bindings has won widespread favor. Wire binding is spun or coiled onto the packet of punched paper ; plastic binding is fastened onto the paper via punched holes by means of a clasping action. Plastic binding

Courtesy: Collamatic, Wayne, N.J.   *Courtesy: Thomas Collators, Inc., New York*

FIG. 53.   The collating machine on the left is electrically operated. A feed roller at each bin ejects one sheet of paper; the operator grasps the sheets, gathers them, and staples each pack with the electric stapler. The unit on the right is an effective hand-operated collator; as many as 32 sheets can be gathered in one continuous operation.

equipment is available for use in the individual office. Such a binding is advantageous in that (1) a variety of different stock—pages, photographs, samples—can be bound together, (2) various page sizes can be securely bound in one manual, (3) revisions and renewals in the manuals can be made conveniently and quickly right in the office, (4) the cost is reasonable, and (5) the binding is sturdy and durable.

SYSTEMS AND PROCEDURES AND DUPLICATING

Duplicating is not limited to making copies that provide convenience but is also an essential component in systems and procedures. In some applications, basic information is put on a master and subsequently duplicated as needed onto paper forms designed to direct and control a particular business activity. For example, in purchasing, master sheets for duplicating can be prepared. When an item is to be purchased, its master is withdrawn from the file, and the needed information duplicated on all the purchasing forms. These forms are then processed, and the master is returned to the file for future use. The result is accurate, fast work and much saving in writing time.

An interesting variation of this procedure is used when several of the requisitions to purchase can be assembled for the preparation of one purchase order for one supplier. The requisitions are sent to the

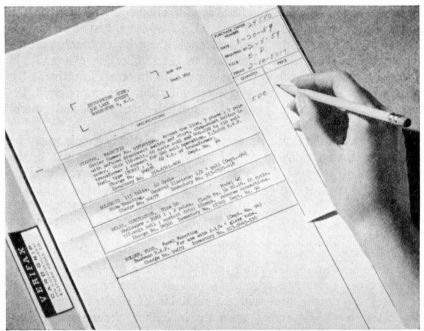

Courtesy: Eastman Kodak Co., Rochester, N.Y.

FIG. 54. Preparation of purchase orders from component parts is expedited by the use of a duplicating machine.

purchasing department, where the buyer groups them respectively under the names of the vendors whom he selects. The card for each selected vendor is removed from the vendor file and assembled with the requisitions which will make up the purchase order to that vendor. These are placed in a shingled or overlapping position and held in place by a large clip. In addition, a variable information form is added, so that the composition of the purchase order can be completed. Figure 54 shows the purchasing requisitions, giving complete specifications, assembled on the left, with the variable information such as purchase order number, date, and quantities being written in on the right. When entries are completed, the entire assembly is placed over a purchasing order master giving heading and shipping instructions—common to all purchase orders—and duplicated. Thus, a complete purchase order is prepared with a minimum of manual writing.

MANAGEMENT OF DUPLICATING WORK

Basic to the management of duplicating work are (1) determining the sequence of the work to be done and (2) deciding what duplicating process to use. Regarding the first, consideration must be given to the urgency of the material; but in general, a first-come, first-serve basis is satisfactory. Grouping the work and establishing its sequence for each duplicating machine gives orderliness to the duplicating efforts. Rigid controls over the issuance of papers are usually in order. Effective is the use of a requisition form showing the duplicating process preferred, the number of copies, size of paper, date needed, destination, and general comments.

Deciding what duplicating process to use is relatively simple when the question is the selection of one of the existing duplicators within the company. To decide what new duplicating machine, if any, should be added brings up the question of what basic types are available, which was discussed above. In addition, what the trends are in duplicating equipment and what choice will best meet the particular requirements, are important.

Duplicating lends itself to a centralized organizational unit. Such an arrangement makes for better utilization of the necessary equipment and machines, encourages adequate supervision, fixes responsibility, and expedites the development and the retaining of efficient operators in duplicating work. Depending upon the individual circumstances, however, duplicating is found as a part of the correspondence organizational section, or whatever unit utilizes duplicating most. Also, in recent years, with the availability of low-cost, easy-to-operate machines, such as those using the contact process giving several copies of letters, billings, or notices that are needed in a hurry, the trend is to disperse these machines throughout the office, placing them at locations where they are used frequently and are convenient to the person needing the copies.

The employee's desire to turn out good quality duplicating work within reasonable periods must be developed and maintained. Basic training is paramount and should include proper use of any equipment utilized. Machine instructions should be given in a step-by-step, easy-to-follow manner and amply illustrated. Many people have the capacity for acquiring acceptable competency, but this ability remains dormant until properly developed through training. It is erroneous and wasteful to place an employee in duplicating and assume that he knows how to do every aspect of the work properly.

All employees need definite work goals but this is especially so for those doing duplicating work. The nature of this work seems to require that a sense of accomplishment be emphasized by its managers. Also the employee's desire to have the manager know what is being achieved must be satisfied. Furthermore, full utilization of the employee's time should be stressed. Too little or too much work can result in a dissatisfied employee. Or expecting the work to be accomplished within practically no time at all can dull the employee's enthusiasm. Team effort is especially urgent because those in duplicating work usually perform several different tasks throughout the day. It is therefore particularly important to maintain a congenial group.

Finally, the controlling efforts over duplicating work should be

DUPLICATING REPORT							
HOURS AND ACTIVITY REPORT			WEEK ENDING				
Regular jobs:			Total paid hours:				
Special jobs:			Time available:				
Machine down time:							
STD. HRS. OPERATION	UNIT	ACTIVITY	STD. HRS.				
			Std.	All.	Taken	Diff.	
Stencils	Stencil		.040				
Run copies	Copy		.00008				
Gather and staple	Copy		.00004				
Plastic binding	Fin. unit		.025				
Material							
20# stock	Ream						

FIG. 55. Comparative data are helpful in controlling the work of duplicating.

thorough and understood by all affected by them. Scheduling of work in economic lot sizes is especially important. The necessary followups to insure delivery of work when processed are likewise essential. The quality of duplicating must be watched to avoid marginal work and that below acceptable levels. Also, it is a good practice to keep an accounting of how much time is spent on each duplicating job. A record such as that shown in Figure 55 assists in these efforts. Reasonable levels of quantity performance should be established and made known to each duplicating employee, so that he knows what is expected of him. The lack of proper duplicating loads per employee is one of the biggest sources of dissatisfaction with poor management of this service. Also, making the duplicating employee cost-conscious about his work is a strong, positive force toward achieving adequate control. However, when corrective action is required, it should be taken immediately.

CHAPTER SIX

CALCULATING
AND COMPARING

To seek the truth for the sake of knowing the truth,
is one of the noblest objects a man can live for.
—*Dean Inge*

OFFICE WORK involving calculating and comparing is present in every enterprise. Figuring of some kind is necessary during the course of normal operations. Costs must be estimated, sales must be added, discounts computed, and interest rates figured. In addition, the data must be compared to insure that the invoices are correct, the calculated quantities balance with each other, and the written copy is accurate. Material requisitions, sales analysis, prorating, percentages, labor distribution, and inventories all require calculating and comparing work.

TYPES OF CALCULATING

In the typical office, adding, subtracting, and multiplying make up the common types of calculating. Studies show that dividing, extracting square root, and solving mathematical formulas constitute a relatively small amount of the total calculating work performed in offices; estimates are that it is some 5 percent of the total calculating work. The tasks involving calculating are many; calculating is required in the preparation of many different types of records.

The preparation of an invoice, for example, requires calculating. As shown in Figure 56, to determine the amount for each item, multiplication or extension work is performed; as indicated, in line 1 of the illustration, three items at $0.62 each equals a total of $1.86 ($3 \times \$0.62$). The sum of these extensions is determined by means of addition. This is illustrated by the amount of $210.74 in the figure. Applying the discount entails subtraction in order to determine the total net amount due. This simple illustration is typical of the need for calculating in order to prepare many common forms of paper work.

MEANS TO USE

In the modern office, much calculating work is done by machine, but other methods are also employed. These include performing the work mentally, working it out in longhand with pencil and paper, utilizing tables and charts of various kinds, and using a slide rule. For convenience, the discussion here will be viewed from (1) the mental or personal basis and (2) the machine basis.

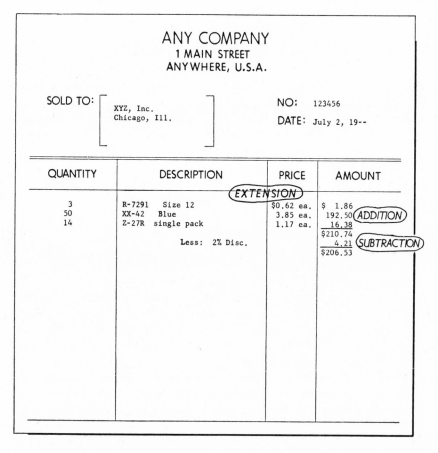

FIG. 56.   Typical calculating work includes extension or multiplication, addition, and subtraction.

CALCULATING BY MENTAL OR PERSONAL BASIS

The personal basis is commonly used for short and relatively simple calculating work. Different methods can be followed; some represent much less work than others. A few effective short cuts will be included here. *In adding a column of figures, it helps to combine pairs or groups of successive numbers that add up to ten.* The addition can proceed from the top down or from the bottom up. For example, to add:

$$5$$
$$3$$
$$7$$
$$6$$
$$3$$
$$1$$
$$4$$

say to yourself (working from top down): 5, 15, 25, 29. The 3 and 7, and the 6, 3, and 1, are grouped as units of 10.

Left-to-right addition is speedy and accurate. This is accomplished by adding the tens of one number to the tens of the next number, then adding the units, and following this pattern successively to the last number. Thus, in order to add:

$$78$$
$$81$$
$$33$$
$$45$$

say 78, 158 (78 + 80), 159 (158 + 1), 189 (159 + 30), 192 (189 + 3), 232 (192 + 40), 237 (232 + 5).

Horizontal addition is helpful in adding numbers not arrayed in column form. Assume the total is wanted from a number of billings, including $42.50, $1.11, $34.77, $9.81, $7.83, $25.40, and $17.08. It is not necessary to arrange the numbers in the form of columns. Simply add the units, then the tens, then the hundreds, and so forth, and write the sums of the successive additions in the form shown below, then add.

Sum of:

Units................	20	(0 + 1 + 7 + 1 + 3 + 0 + 8)
Tens.................	33	(5 + 1 + 7 + 8 + 8 + 4 + 0)
Hundreds...........	35	(2 + 1 + 4 + 9 + 7 + 5 + 7)
Thousands..........	10	(4 + 3 + 2 + 1)
Total.............	$138.50	

Multiplication by near number is simple, yet it is not commonly practiced. By this procedure multiplying quickly by numbers near 10, 100, or 1,000 is possible. For example, 368 multiplied by $0.98 consists of

$$
\begin{array}{rl}
368 \text{ times } \$1.00 = & \$368.00 \\
\text{less } 368 \text{ times } \;\; 0.02 = & \underline{\;\;\;7.36} \\
& \$360.64
\end{array}
$$

In other words, multiplying by 100 is accomplished by simply adding two zeros to the end of the number being multiplied, then adjusting this figure for the amount the multiplier deviates from 100. In like manner, if the multiplier had been $0.12, the multiplier used would be 10 and the calculation would be

$$
\begin{array}{rl}
368 \text{ times } \$0.10 = & \$36.80 \\
\text{plus } 368 \text{ times } \;\; 0.02 = & \underline{\;\;\;7.36} \\
& \$44.16
\end{array}
$$

The breakdown method of multiplication is a time-saver when the personal method of calculating is followed. Actually, this is similar to multiplication by near number and differs in degree, not in type. To multiply by 50, for example, multiply by 100, which is easily done, and take one-half, since 50 is one-half of 100. Likewise, to multiply by 25, take one-fourth of that found by multiplying by 100. To illustrate, $1.95 times 25 equals one-fourth of $195.00, or $48.75. In multiplying $1.95 times 26, an additional amount for one unit, or $1.95, would be added to $48.75, giving $50.70.

The use of reciprocals represents another short cut. A reciprocal of a number is one divided by that number, i.e., the reciprocal of four is one-fourth. Calculating work involving percentages and prorating can be expedited by the use of reciprocals because dividing by a number is the same as multiplying by the reciprocal of that number. Assume from the following data that percentage figures are to be calculated:

Department	Sales	Percentage Total
A	$ 3,905.40	
B	7,041.62	
C	2,052.98	
Total	$13,000.00	100.00%

The reciprocal of 13,000.00 is 0.000076923. Multiplying the sales for each department by this reciprocal gives the respective percentages of 30.04, 54.17, and 15.79. Normally a table of reciprocals is used to simplify the work. Figure 57 shows the reciprocals for numbers 1–20, inclusive. In many cases, even though machines are employed, the use of reciprocals for this type of calculating is followed. It makes division possible when the machine adds and multiplies only. Also, in some cases it is deemed desirable to have the operator stay with multiplying work only, that is, not mix the work of multiplying with that of dividing.

Number	Reciprocal	Number	Reciprocal
1......	1.000000	11.......	0.090909
2.	0.500000	12..... .	0.083333
3.	0.333333	13.	0.076923
4.......	0.250000	14.. .	0.071428
5.......	0.200000	15.......	0.066666
6..	0.166666	16. .	0.062500
7......	0.142857	17.......	0.058823
8.......	0.125000	18.. ...	0.055555
9.......	0.111111	19.......	0.052631
10.	0.100000	20.......	0.050000

FIG. 57. Numbers from 1–20, inclusive, and their reciprocals.

Calculating of discounts is another area where short cuts can be used. Among the important discounts and the reason for granting them are:

Discount	Reason
Quantity:	Less expensive to handle large orders
Trade:	Different types of buyers perform different marketing functions
Cash:	Inducement for prompt payment

Customarily, a full or list price is used as the base from which the discount or discounts are applied. When two or more discounts are in effect, each is applied to the net amount remaining after the previous discount has been taken. For example, with a list price of $25.00 and discounts of 30 percent and 10 percent, denoted as 30 and 10, the net price is $15.75, calculated as follows:

```
List price............................$25.00
Less 30% (first discount)...............  7.50
Balance...............................$17.50
Less 10% (second discount)............  1.75
Net price.............................$15.75
```

This method is too cumbersome. A simpler method follows. A 30 percent discount means 70 percent (100 − 30) remains; hence, the amount can be determined by multiplying the list price by 70 percent. Likewise, a 10 percent discount means 90 percent applies. In the above example, the calculation is therefore

$$\$25.00 \times 0.70 \times 0.90 = \$15.75.$$

Another simple method is to determine the single rate equal to the two discounts. To do this, add the discounts and subtract the sum obtained by multiplying the discounts:

$$0.30 + 0.10 = 0.40$$
$$\text{less } 0.30 \times 0.10 = \underline{0.03}$$
$$\text{Equivalent discount } = \overline{0.37}$$

or $(1.00 - 0.37)$ remains, applying to $25.00 equals:

$$0.63 \times \$25.00, \text{ or } \$15.75.$$

Where the calculating work includes various discounts, it is common practice to make up a table showing the equivalent single discount and the net that is applicable. Such a table is illustrated by Figure 58.

Discount percent	Equivalent	Net
10.....................	0.10	0.90
10 & 5.................	0.145	0.855
10, 5, & 5.............	0.1878	0.8122
20.....................	0.20	0.80
20 & 10...............	0.28	0.72
20, 10, & 5...........	0.316	0.684
40.....................	0.40	0.60
40 & 5.................	0.43	0.57
40, 5, & 10...........	0.487	0.513
40, 10, & 5...........	0.487	0.513
50.....................	0.50	0.50
50, 10, & 10..........	0.595	0.405

FIG. 58. Discounts, their equivalents, and net amounts.

CALCULATING BY MACHINE BASIS

Modern office machines have reduced calculating work to very simple tasks. Lengthy columns of figures can be added in a matter of seconds; and if wanted, a written record is available for checking the accuracy or for future reference. Errors due to handwriting figures incorrectly, carelessly, or out of column are eliminated by the machine basis. We will discuss adding machines and calculating machines.

Adding machines are basically of two types: key-driven and crank-driven. In the former case, the machine mechanism is actuated by depressing a key; in the latter case, the number is "put in the machine" by depressing the key, and the mechanism is actuated by pulling a lever or pressing a motor bar. These two basic types are subject to important variations, including listing or nonlisting, full keyboard or ten-keyboard, and manual or electric.

A listing machine lists or produces a written record of the figures on a tape. This can serve as a machine record, for visual comparison, or as proof of work. Where a long column of numbers, over a hundred, for example, is involved, a listing is usually desired. However, when a

Courtesy: Monroe Calculating Machine Co., Inc., Orange, N.J.   Courtesy: Burroughs Corp., Detroit

FIG. 59.   Adding machines. *Left:* Listing ten-key model. *Right:* Listing full-keyboard, ten-column-capacity machine.

nonlisting machine is used and proof of work is required, the work can be checked by going through the addition twice and comparing answers. In some instances, this method is as quick as checking a tape record.

A full-keyboard machine provides a column of keys from 1 to 9 for each digit position. Thus, a five-row machine can handle a number like 628.47. The full keyboard permits high speeds where numbers of four or less digits are involved, because the keys can be depressed simultaneously. A ten-keyboard type has, as the name suggests, ten keys from 0 to 9. Within the machine capacity, all numbers are recorded by means of these ten keys. The number 629.43 would be handled by first presssing the key 6, then 2, and then 9, and so on until the number is completed. The ten-key machine is usually very satisfactory for large numbers. The hand travel is small, since it is confined to ten keys. Numbers with five or more digits are quickly handled on this machine.

The names *manual* and *electric* are self-explanatory, but in both cases the keys are depressed by hand. The manual usually has lower maintenance cost, is lighter, and no electric cords are necessary; the machine can be operated anywhere. In contrast, the electric machine is faster and saves the operator's energy; however, its initial cost is usually greater. Most adding machines can also be used for subtracting, and a number are adaptable for work involving multiplying and dividing. Illustrations of several different types of adding machines are shown by Figure 59.

Calculating machines are specially built for multiplication and division work, which is really repetitive addition and subtraction, respectively; that is, 3 times 3 is the same as 3 plus 3 plus 3, and 9 divided by 3 is equal to the number of times 3 can be subtracted from 9, i.e., 9 less 3, less 3, less 3. The same considerations apply to calculators as discussed above under adding machines.

Among the latest calculating machines is the Victor 3900 Electronic Calculator which displays its work progress on a built-in 4 x 2½-inch illuminating display screen. Up to 30 digit figures can be accommodated and multiplying, dividing, adding, and subtracting can be performed in a wink. The machine features very quiet operation—you have to see it to believe it's working—and five display registers, three of which are calculating registers and two are storage registers. The independent memory unit of the machine stores any factor at the touch of a key and brings it back to the processing register at the touch of another key. Figure 60 shows this machine.

A fully automatic calculator with simplified listing is shown by Figure 61. In multiplying or in dividing, there is no repetition of figures on the tape—just the problem and the answer, as shown in the upper left of the figure. This machine is available with capacity up to $1 trillion. There is also available

Courtesy: Victor Comptometer Corp., Chicago

FIG. 60. The Victor 3900 Electronic Calculator which is accurate, incredibly fast, and shows its work on an illuminated screen which is a part of the unit.

a listing calculator featuring a wide range of application, high speed, and interoperation transfers, making it possible to perform sequences of combined operations such as storing data in the machine and recalling for use in subsequent operations. An illustration of this machine and several examples of the calculating work it can perform are shown by Figure 62.

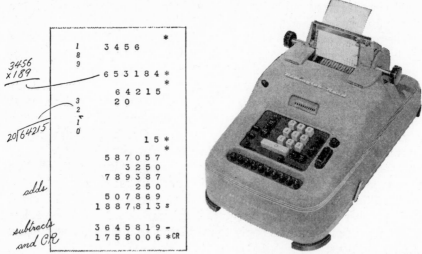

Courtesy: Remington Rand, Inc., New York

FIG. 61. A fully automatic printing calculator, with an example of its work.

THE OFFICE WORK OF COMPARING

Reading handwritten or typed copy and columns of numbers for accuracy accounts for a sizable portion of office workers' time. Progress in reducing these comparing efforts for checking purposes has been made, as evidenced by proofing masters only of duplicated material, personal basis shortcuts for checking calculations, and proofing devices on office machines. For the most part, material to be checked falls into two categories: (1) material that requires exact comparison with the original and (2) material that necessitates general checking for correctness of intended meaning and satisfactory appearance.

When exact comparison is required, it is common for one employee to read from the original while another employee checks the material. A word-for-word comparison is made. The employee reading indicates headings, quotations, and punctuation marks, and spells difficult words. Care must be exercised by the employee checking to catch omissions, misspelled words, and incorrect syllabifications. Along with this, an examination is made to see that the general format, margins, and appearance are correct.

In checking numbers read the columns vertically. Place the original list side by side with the written list, so that the numbers are matched on the same line. This helps to eliminate possible error. The doubling of figures and using the comma division should also be practiced whenever possible.

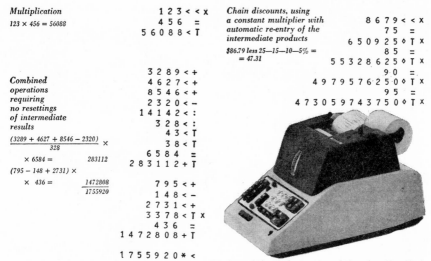

Multiplication

123 × 456 = 56088

```
    1 2 3 < < x
      4 5 6   =
  5 6 0 8 8 < T
```

*Combined
operations
requiring
no resettings
of intermediate
results*

$$\frac{(3289 + 4627 + 8546 - 2320)}{328} \times$$

×6584 =   283112

(795 − 148 + 2731) ×

× 436 =   1472808
               1755920

```
    3 2 8 9 < +
    4 6 2 7 < +
    8 5 4 6 < +
    2 3 2 0 < −
  1 4 1 4 2 < :
      3 2 8 < :
        4 3 < T
        3 8 < T
      6 5 8 4   =
  2 8 3 1 1 2 + T

      7 9 5 < +
      1 4 8 < −
    2 7 3 1 < +
    3 3 7 8 < T x
      4 3 6   =
  1 4 7 2 8 0 8 + T

  1 7 5 5 9 2 0 * <
```

*Chain discounts, using
a constant multiplier with
automatic re-entry of the
intermediate products*

*$86.79 less 25—15—10—5% =
        = 47.31*

```
        8 6 7 9 < < x
              7 5   =
      6 5 0 9 2 5 ◊ T x
              8 5   =
    5 5 3 2 8 6 2 5 ◊ T x
              9 0   =
    4 9 7 9 5 7 6 2 5 0 ◊ T x
              9 5   =
  4 7 3 0 5 9 7 4 3 7 5 0 ◊ T x
```

Courtesy: Olivetti Corporation of America, New York

FIG. 62. A listing automatic calculator with a wide range of applications. Illustrations of the printed tape supplied by the machine are shown.

For numbers that repeat, use the expression "two times," "three times," and so forth. To illustrate:

When the number is:	*Say:*
157	One fifty-seven
2157	Twenty-one fifty-seven
2,157	Two one fifty-seven
3,845,157	Three eight forty-five one fifty-seven
341⎫ 341⎬ 341⎭	Three forty-one —three times

Material requiring general checking is carefully read, but a word-for-word comparison is not made. Frequently, general checking work is done by one employee—commonly the one who wrote the material. The meaning of the material must be clear and the general appearance satisfactory. Special attention should be given dates and amounts. In this respect, comparison with the original is recommended.

UNIT ANALYSIS COMPARATIVE REPORTS

The summarizing of much data in a neat and concise form emphasizing comparisons describes the unit analysis comparative report which is illustrated by Figure 63. The data are written on specially designed forms held in place by binder rings through holes at the top of each form.

PERIOD JANUARY THIS YEAR	PERIOD FEBRUARY THIS YEAR	PERIOD MARCH THIS YEAR	PERIOD APRIL LAST YEAR	PERIOD APRIL THIS YEAR	OPERATING REPORT	% OF SALES	TO DATE APRIL THIS YEAR
					SALES		
60,125	62,411	63,147	51,675	57,355	PRODUCT A	55.2	243,038
51,312	61,387	62,298	44,375	55,467	PRODUCT B	44.8	230,464
111,437	123,798	125,445	96,050	112,822	TOTAL	100.0	473,502
					COST OF SALES		
42,066	42,439	43,571	35,643	41,296	PRODUCT A	69.9	169,371
35,462	43,279	43,921	30,234	38,272	PRODUCT B	70.0	160,934
77,528	85,718	87,492	65,877	79,567	TOTAL	70.0	330,305
					GROSS PROFIT		
18,059	19,972	19,576	16,032	18,060	PRODUCT A	30.1	73,667
15,850	18,108	18,377	14,141	17,195	PRODUCT B	30.0	69,530
33,909	38,080	37,953	30,173	33,255	TOTAL	30.0	143,197
					COST OF SALES ADJUSTMENTS		
1,211	657	752	418	456	INVENTORY ADJUSTMENTS		3,076
2,075	1,947	1,846	1,157	1,411	OVER OR UNDER ABSORBED BURDEN		7,279
3,286	2,604	2,598	1,575	1,867	TOTAL	1.9	10,355
30,623	35,476	35,355	28,598	31,388	GROSS PROFIT AFTER ADJ.	28.1	132,842
					GENERAL EXPENSES		
6,317	7,185	7,321	5,732	6,930	ADMINISTRATIVE – SCHEDULE A		27,753
8,245	9,345	8,560	7,048	6,742	SELLING – SCHEDULE B		32,892
3,612	4,762	5,121	3,848	4,637	SHIPPING – SCHEDULE C		18,132
2,098	2,417	2,860	2,461	2,420	BRANCH – SCHEDULE D		9,795
20,272	23,709	23,862	19,089	20,729	TOTAL EXPENSES	18.7	88,572
10,351	11,767	11,493	9,509	10,659	NET PROFIT FROM OPERATIONS	9.4	44,270
					OTHER INCOME		
251	187	252	142	210	INTEREST EARNED		900
516	518	675	567	572	DISCOUNT ON PURCHASES		2,281
122	158	145		112	DIVIDENDS RECEIVED		537
		250			PROFIT ON SALE OF ASSETS		250
218					PROFIT ON SALE OF INVESTMENTS		218
1,107	863	1,322	709	894	TOTAL OTHER INCOME	.9	4,186
					OTHER DEDUCTIONS		
376	112	87	123	75	INTEREST PAID		650
678	458	567	482	420	DISCOUNT ON SALES		2,123
	100				LOSS ON SALE OF ASSETS		100
					LOSS ON SALE OF INVESTMENTS		
1,054	670	654	605	495	TOTAL OTHER DEDUCTIONS	.6	2,873
53	193	668	104	399	NET	.3	1,313
10,404	11,960	12,161	9,613	11,058	NET PROFIT BEFORE TAXES	9.7	45,583
					TAXES		
55	55	55	45	55	CAPITAL STOCK		220
145	152	159	127	121	STATE INCOME		577
3,675	3,742	3,815	2,655	3,420	FEDERAL INCOME		14,652
3,875	3,949	4,029	2,827	3,596	TOTAL TAXES	3.1	15,449
6,529	8,011	8,132	6,786	7,	NET PROFIT FROM ALL SOURCES	6.6	30,134

JUST LIFT UP

Courtesy: Royal-McBee Co., New York

FIG. 63.   Comparative and accumulative operating and financial information is presented in an effective arrangement.

TO DATE APRIL LAST YEAR	TO DATE MAY LAST YEAR	TO DATE JUNE LAST YEAR	TO DATE JULY LAST YEAR	TO DATE AUGUST LAST YEAR	TO DATE SEPT. LAST YEAR	TO DATE OCTOBER LAST YEAR	TO DATE NOVEMBER LAST YEAR	TO DATE DECEMBER LAST YEAR
212,966	265,648	322,377	380,739	441,106	506,089	576,913	651,284	716,671
195,033	238,744	286,557	334,678	387,159	442,183	501,494	559,179	615,890
407,999	504,392	608,934	715,417	828,265	948,272	1078,407	1210,463	1332,561
150,092	188,548	228,527	271,129	313,991	358,719	407,341	458,628	503,750
138,676	168,147	202,572	238,256	272,467	310,328	351,012	390,713	429,433
286,768	356,695	431,099	507,385	586,458	668,147	758,353	849,341	933,183
62,874	77,100	93,850	109,610	127,115	147,370	169,572	192,656	212,921
58,357	70,597	83,985	98,422	114,692	131,855	150,482	168,466	186,457
121,231	147,697	177,835	208,032	241,807	279,225	320,054	361,122	399,378
1,723	2,234	2,711	3,161	3,886	4,268	4,822	5,643	6,284
4,318	5,578	6,735	7,815	9,199	10,360	11,676	12,894	13,881
6,041	7,812	9,446	10,976	13,085	14,628	16,498	18,537	20,145
115,190	139,885	168,389	197,056	228,722	264,597	303,556	342,585	379,233
21,908	27,338	32,972	38,783	44,604	50,539	56,786	63,284	69,205
27,909	34,726	41,868	48,805	55,740	62,860	70,244	77,826	84,741
15,607	19,327	22,846	26,691	30,515	34,283	38,450	42,837	46,757
10,361	12,933	15,249	17,787	20,734	24,878	29,328	34,483	39,569
75,783	94,324	112,935	132,046	151,593	172,560	194,808	218,430	240,272
39,407	45,561	55,454	65,010	77,129	92,037	108,748	124,155	138,961
541	707	853	1,035	1,228	1,400	1,581	1,737	1,864
2,081	2,773	3,288	3,900	4,525	5,337	6,102	6,724	7,439
110	110	110	110	325	465	595	595	595
163	163	163	163	287	287	287	487	487
251	251	251	251	251	251	251	251	251
3,146	4,004	4,665	5,459	6,616	7,740	8,816	9,794	10,636
505	615	702	817	911	1,021	1,206	1,378	1,535
1,680	2,055	2,483	3,045	3,583	4,085	4,647	5,372	5,993
215	215	215	215	361	361	361	361	361
2,380	2,885	3,400	4,077	4,855	5,447	6,214	7,111	7,889
766	1,119	1,265	1,382	1,761	2,293	2,602	2,683	2,747
40,173	46,680	56,719	66,392	78,890	94,330	111,350	126,838	141,708
180	225	270	315	375	430	498	570	637
479	601	725	850	1,002	1,183	1,377	1,587	1,774
11,107	13,687	16,504	18,685	22,103	25,791	29,813	34,093	37,958
11,766	14,513	17,499	19,850	23,480	27,404	31,688	36,250	40,369
28,407	32,167	39,220	46,542	55,410	66,926	79,662	90,588	101,339

At the close of each period, such as a month, the data for the current month are posted in the left-hand column of a strip and the year to date figures in the right-hand column; the center of the strip is used for identifying information. By properly positioning the newly completed monthly strip in the binder, comparisons between figures for the current month and those of previous periods are supplied. In the illustration, for example, comparisons are expedited between (1) April this year and previous months of this year, (2) April this year and April last year, and (3) the year to date this month with the same period last year. The unit analysis method assists in presenting calculated data in a convenient and usable pattern, in determining trends, measuring the efficiency of the operations, and highlighting the status of different components making up the entire activity.

PEGBOARD AND PAPER STRIPS

Pegboard accounting, also known as shingle-strip and summary-strip accounting, is another type of strip arrangement for accumulating or summarizing a large number of items with minimum time, maximum accuracy, and convenience. The equipment consists of a special board and ready-made paper strips, about 2 to 3 inches wide and 16 inches long, fastened to the board. Original data are written on the strips. These strips are held in alignment by means of holes across the top which fit into a peg strip at the top of the board. The arrangement of the paper strips is offset so that a vertical margin of each strip is exposed, thus disclosing a column of figures. Quick summaries and "recaps" can be run off. A movable horizontal bar is used to guide the eye to the proper line across the forms.

Pegboard accounting is particularly effective in making distribution analyses of various kinds, including cost, payroll, stock control, and sales, and it can be designed to serve almost every type of business. The boards are made in various sizes, ranging from approximately 20 x 18 inches to 36 x 18 inches. The advantages of the use of peg strips include the following: Copying of the data is eliminated—the original forms are used to obtain final results; accurate information can be provided; flexibility is permitted, since variations in the number and kind of distributions are possible; and the cost is economical—there is a minimum of handling, and the equipment required is simple.

To cite a specific example, a chain of stores selling poultry uses a pegboard master summary sheet about 16 inches by 17½ inches to get the totals of all inventories left over at the end of the week in each store as well as a comparison of the inventories with the week's orders. Individual order-inventory reports for various stores are posted on the master sheet. These postings are recorded on smaller forms in back of the master and so registered that a column of red spot carbon is used for data on inventories and black spot carbon for week's orders. A separate small form is used for each store. When all the postings have been made, the smaller forms are shingled into position and it is an easy matter to add all the red figures across the line to determine the total by items for left-over inventories and all the black figures for week's orders.

MANAGERIAL CONSIDERATIONS OF CALCULATING AND COMPARING

Calculating and comparing are normally organized on a decentralized basis because they are common to many office jobs. However, where volume of work warrants, it is satisfactory to have a centralized computing or comparing group, which is usually a part of the organization unit having the largest quantity of these types of work—probably the bookkeeping section.

Calculating requires employees with a *number sense,* that is, an ability to recognize relations that exist between numbers and to think of numbers in their broad relations. Placing this type of person in calculating work will bring the best results. Comparing is detailed, repetitive work and requires reading skill, patience, and a passion for accuracy. Proper personnel selection for comparing work will greatly strengthen the organization utilized.

Basic training is paramount to secure proficiency in calculating and comparing work. Many people have the background for acquiring acceptable competency, but this ability is never developed unless effective training is applied. Proper operation of machines used is also important for use of the machine is limited by knowledge of the operator. The machine does only what the operator has it do. Instructional material is helpful; but to provide maximum benefits, it should be prepared in a step-by-step, easy-to-follow plan, and amply illustrated. It takes practice and a sincere determination to perform either calculating or comparing work speedily and competently. The techniques must be understood, but skill in applying them is essential.

As in most office services, a key consideration is having an adequate amount of work scheduled to each employee doing calculating or comparing work. The load should be fair and reasonable and clearly understood by the employee. Not only does this establish good work relationships, but it also provides for each employee work targets which are fundamental to efficient management.

CHAPTER SEVEN

FILING

*When a man's knowledge is not in order,
the more of it he has the greater will be his confusion.*
—Herbert Spencer

To HELP provide information when needed, data are stored according to some arrangement so that they are readily available. In the normal course of business, reference to written information concerning plans, decisions, thoughts, contracts, obligations, drawings, research, and transactions is utilized quite frequently. To supply this needed office service requires filing, which can be defined as follows: *Filing is the placing of papers in acceptable containers according to some predetermined arrangement so that any paper, when required, can be located quickly and conveniently.* Emphasis is upon the "finding," not the "storing" aspect. Placing the information in safekeeping is important; being able to find it promptly, when wanted, is vital. One needed paper lost or mislaid can delay a dozen employees in their work.

FILING—IMPORTANCE AND ARRANGEMENT

Each year, greater quantities of papers must be filed; and the problem of how best to handle them for quick reference, what arrangement to follow, what policies to adopt, and what equipment to utilize multiplies the need for competent office managerial action. The office is unique in that it stores many of its "products." This is a necessary part of its service. As we create more records, demand more information, and require more controls, filing has grown in importance. Every record and paper created and processed must have proper disposition. If it does not, or if we permit nonessential and excessive papers to be produced and filed, we are adding to the problem of filing. Fundamental are the facts that (1) filing is an integral part of paper work processing and (2) when searching for information, there should be as few places as possible to look, preferably only one.

The type of material handled, the nature and size of the enterprise, and the peculiarities of the particular business influence the selection of the arrangement of papers in the file. Numerous ready-made filing arrangements are offered on the market. Different manufacturers stress different features. The arrangement selected should provide for distinct divisions of the material, allow for possible expansion, and be inclusive of all the material to be handled.

There are four basic filing arrangements: (1) alphabetical, (2) numerical, (3) geographical, (4) chronological. Various modifications and combinations of these are possible and, in fact, are commonly used. For example, subject filing by an alphabetical arrangement is widely used, an alphabetical-numerical plan is often employed; and in many alphabetical files, the material in each subdivision is arranged chronologically, i.e., the latest paper always on top. Likewise, under the geographical plan it is customary to arrange the subdivisions alphabetically.

ALPHABETICAL FILING

The alphabetical arrangement, or some modification of it, is the most widely used form of filing. It stresses the name or topic as the important

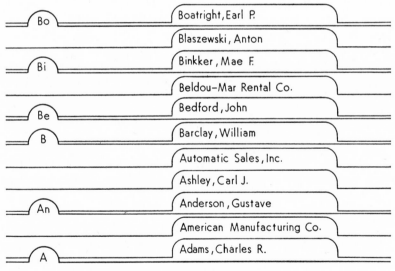

FIG. 64. Alphabetical filing.

item. The filing is by dictionary order. If the first letter is not sufficient for determining the proper place of the material, the second and, if necessary, the third and fourth succeeding letters are used. See Figure 64. For any given total of names, the probable number which will occur in each subdivision of the alphabet is known. For example, names beginning with the letters *S*, *B*, *M*, and *H*, respectively, are most common; those beginning with *X*, *Q*, and *U* occur least frequently. For a given quantity of names, there are usually about three times as many names under *B* as under *A*, twenty times as many under *H* as under *I*, and ten times as many under *T* as under *U*. Information of this sort is utilized scientifically in determining filing guide subdivisions, which can be purchased as standard equipment. Sets ranging from 24 to some 2,600 subdivisions are available.

To provide for expansion, sets are available that permit the inserting of additional subdivisions to the original set. For example, a set of 300 subdivisions is converted into one of 400 subdivisions simply by adding an expansion package of 100 subdivisions. None of the original subdivisions are discarded; there is no waste.

The advantages of alphabetical filing are that direct reference is provided, a quick check is offered on misfiled material, and common names are grouped. It is sometimes considered "the natural way to file." Figure 65 illustrates a modern alphabetical filing arrangement for correspondence. From this illustration, the following can be observed:

1. The primary guides, or partitions segregating the material, give the chief breakdowns of the alphabet and are identified by green tabs occupying the first three positions which are shown along the top left portion of the guide.[1] These tabs are marked with letters and numbers, i.e., $A = 1$, $Abr = 2$, $Ad = 3$, $Ag = 4$, etc. The number expedites the filing work. When considering the letter *d*, it is a little difficult to recall that *d* is between *c* and *e*. In contrast, no thought is required to remember that the number 3 is between 2 and 4.

2. Individual folders containing regular correspondence are filed behind their proper primary guide and tabbed in the fifth or extreme right position: "1. Aaron, Carl"; "1. Abbott, A. M."; etc.

3. Miscellaneous folders, used for occasional and miscellaneous correspondence, are marked with red tabs in the first three positions. These folders correspond in identification and number with the primary guides and are placed in the back of each primary-guide spacing. When regular material is moved to the transfer file, the miscellaneous folders are moved also and serve as primary guides in this file.[2]

4. Auxiliary guides, tabbed in the fourth or right-center position, are used to simplify and to speed the filing by dividing primary-guide spacings

---

[1] Tabs are located by position along the width of the guide. At the left is the first position, and moving to the right are the second, third, fourth, and fifth positions; the fifth position is at the extreme right.

[2] The transfer of filed material is discussed in Chapter 8.

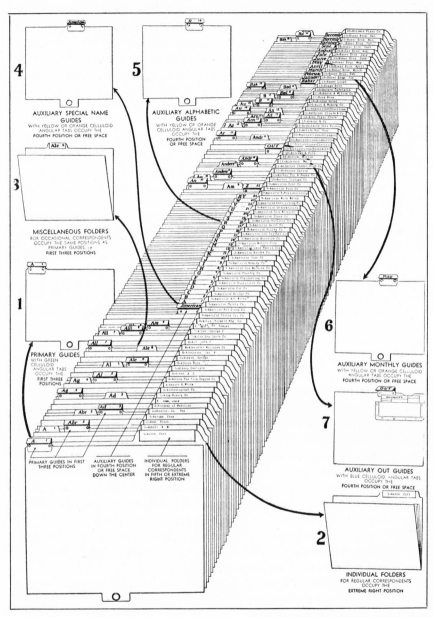

Courtesy: Globe-Wernicke Co., Cincinnati, O.

FIG. 65.   Filing arrangement under a modern alphabetical correspondence filing plan.

according to individual needs. Auxiliary guides may include (*a*) common titles and names, such as "American," "Brown," "Smith," and "United States"; (*b*) alphabetical listings which segregate the material under the common title or name—"American Art Works" or "American Bridge Co.," for example; and (*c*) monthly listings which separate the material under the common title or name by months—"Baker Bros.—Jan.," "Baker Bros.—Feb.," and "Baker Bros.—March."

5. Out guides are tabbed with blue in the fourth position and are inserted in the file when any folder is taken out. Each out guide is equipped with a holder device for a charge-out card. Entries on this card show when a folder is removed, by whom, and when returned. Out guides are also available in folder form, in which case spaces are ruled on the side in order to record data on removals.[3]

It will be of interest to note here that tabs for file guides are available in several types and, to expedite filing, the top of file folders are cut in a choice of various "positions." See Figure 66.

SUBJECT FILING

A modification of the alphabetical arrangement is subject filing, in which the arrangement of material is according to subject or descriptive feature instead of name. For example, all material pertaining to insurance is put in one main division and all material on taxes in another division. If necessary, subdivisions of each subject are made. For Insurance, the subdivisions might be Accident, Fire, and Group; and the material is usually filed alphabetically under each classification. The choice of subject heading should be inclusive and descriptive of the contents. Any logical grouping based on usage is permissible. Idiomatic terminology should be used. If employees habitually ask for the file on Employment, it is not helpful to insist upon filing such material under Applications for Employment.

Subject filing helps to indicate the main classifications for separate files in an office. To illustrate, a separate file may be used for each main subject, such as costs, orders, personal, purchases, and taxes. Subheadings are included under each main subject, for example, under Orders are Adjustments, Collections, Complaints, Correspondence, and Shipments. In addition, subject filing places all material of a common descriptive feature together, so that it can be used conveniently. Common examples of subject filing include executive files, files of material going between home office

---

[3] The subject of charging material out is discussed on page 122.

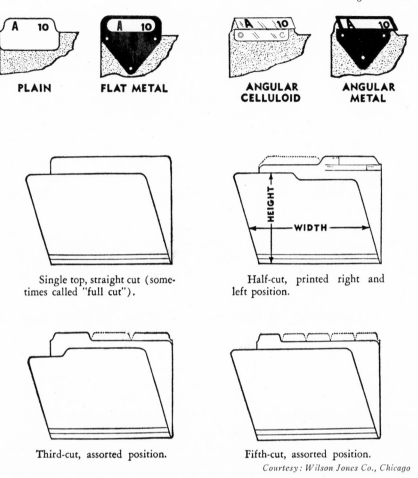

FIG. 66. *Top:* Styles of tabs for file guides. *Bottom:* Offset cuts at top of file folders.

and branches, interdepartmental written material, research data, clippings, and notes.

PHONETIC FILING

Another interesting modification of the alphabetical arrangement is phonetic filing. In many instances, a name can be spelled in different ways. For example, the name "Barnett" can also be spelled "Barnet," "Bornet," "Bornett," and so forth. Under which spelling is such a name filed or found? Poor handwriting and errors in transcribing might add further to the filing perplexity. To meet this problem, a system of file indexing based on the pronunciation or sound of the name has been developed.

Under this system, all names are coded by use of the "Soundex Code," which is:

Code Numbers	Key Letter Equivalents
1	*b, f, p, v*
2	*c, g, j, k, q, s, x, z*
3	*d, t*
4	*l*
5	*m, n*
6	*r*

The letters *a, e, i, o, u* and *w, h, y* are not coded. In addition, the following practices apply:

1. The initial letter is not coded but is used as a prefix to code a number which always has three digits.
2. The zero is used where there is no key letter equivalent.
3. Doubled key letters are coded as one, that is, *rr* as *r*.
4. A key letter and its equivalent are likewise coded as one, that is, *ck* as *c*.

To illustrate, the name "Barnett" would be coded B—653; "Barnet," B—653; and "Bornet," B—653. Thus, all names which sound alike, although spelled differently, have an identical filing location and thus can be quickly located. A phonetic filing system is a special type of alphabetic-numeric arrangement. Among the important advantages of phonetic indexing are the following: Ninety percent of all family names are grouped automatically, duplications are detected, unlimited expansion and flexibility are provided, the effect of transcribing errors is minimized, and a uniform and precise indexing method is provided.

NUMERICAL FILING

In this filing arrangement, each item filed has a number, and location of the material is by numerical sequence. Numerical files are used for such material as bank checks, invoices, engine numbers, and papers pertaining to freight cars. However, the numerical arrangement is not confined to prenumbered material. Items such as letters, memorandums, and notices are also filed according to this plan; and in such cases, an auxiliary alphabetical card file is employed to learn the proper filing number. The system of numbers can be basically one of two types: (1) serial—to provide unlimited expansion, or (2) coded—to indicate specific types of items. An illustration of the latter type is given below:

Divisions

100. *General Sales*	200. *Production*	300. *Research*
110. Recap of orders booked	210. Purchasing	310. Consumer studies
120. Recap of sales shipped	220. Payroll	320. Radio ratings
130. Expenditures	230. Budget	330. Television surveys
140. Budget	240. Recap of items completed	340. Readership records
		350. Product testing

The numerical plan offers simple provisions for expansion, some degree of secrecy, ease and speed of operation, and an effective means of identification. Numbers are easy to work with; in fact, most alphabetical filing systems use numbers on the file guides, in addition to the letters, in

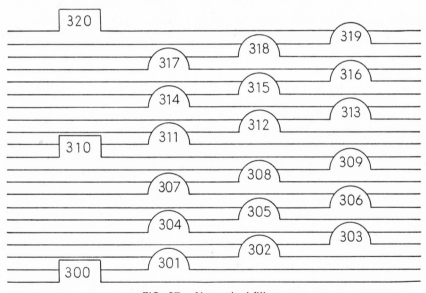

FIG. 67. Numerical filing.

order to expedite finding. Figure 67 shows the arrangement of a numerical file.

In terminal-digit filing, a variation of regular numerical filing, numbers are used, but they are read from right to left instead of the conventional left to right. Hence, records are filed according to the last digit or, more commonly, the last two digits, then the next two or subdivision thereof. To illustrate:

In Numerical File	In Terminal-Digit File Last-Two Number Breakdown	In Terminal-Digit File Last-Two Number Breakdown with Sub-divisions Thereof
160 79	3 25 41	5 17 41
174 63	5 17 41	3 25 41
325 41	1 74 63	1 74 63
517 41	1 60 79	1 60 79

Why file this way? To eliminate misfiles from misreading six or more digits, as happens in regular numerical filing, and to disperse filing activity —the newest records are not placed at one end of the file, causing congested activity in that part of the file.

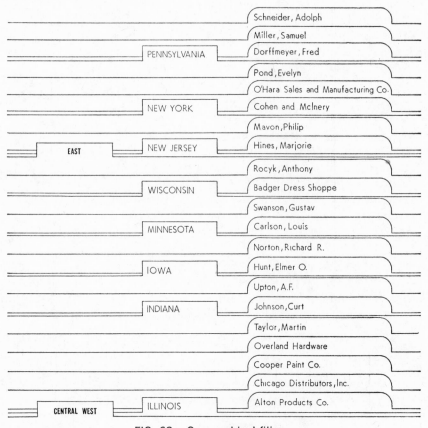

FIG. 68. Geographical filing.

GEOGRAPHICAL FILING

The main filing divisions in the geographical arrangement include states, counties, cities, branch-office territories, and salesmen's areas. Usually, the subdivisions are arranged alphabetically; for example, a sales area by cities in alphabetic order, and each city by customers' names in alphabetic order.

The geographical arrangement, sometimes called location arrangement, is easy to understand, simple and direct, and can cover the over-all work division, particularly that of sales. The files are generally less unwieldy than is frequently the case with the other basic arrangements. Also, several people can work at the files simultaneously—for instance, one in the Philadelphia file for "Cupper Manufacturing Company" and the other in the Los Angeles file for "Cizzla Sales Corporation." In addition, the geographical arrangement makes it comparatively simple to compile mailing lists by states or cities; and the segregation of material for tax, political, or mailing reasons is readily provided. Figure 68 shows a geographical plan of filing.

CHRONOLOGICAL FILING

The chronological filing arrangement simply arranges material according to its time sequence. The main divisions are either months or weeks, with the subdivisions being days. Some correspondence, bills, and pending accounts payable can be handled on a chronological plan. The advantages of this plan are simplicity, ease of filing, and a convenient signal or reminder of unfinished work, which is shown by the material in the file with reference to a specific date. Figure 69 illustrates chronological filing.

The "tickler file" is an adaptation of chronological filing. Future matters requiring attention are filed under due dates or the time when action should be taken. A glance at the file shows for any given period what matters are to be followed up, what ones are behind schedule, and what ones must be handled in the near future.

FILE INDEXING

The file index furnishes the key to how the materials are arranged. For any given set of material, a choice is made from several possible indexes. In some cases, the subject is the best index; in others, the name of the customer or the point of destination might be most useful. To illustrate,

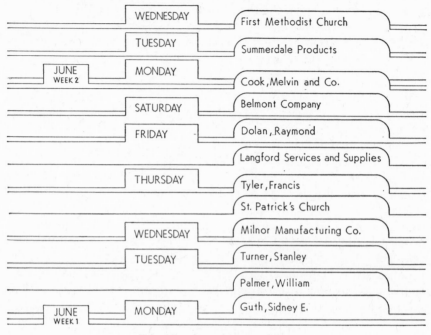

FIG. 69.   Chronological filing.

the following material could be indexed in any one of the several different ways indicated:

Material	File according to:
Catalogs	Date, name of company, or name of product
Correspondence	Date, subject, name of company, name of customer, name of seller, point of destination, or point of origin
Invoices	Date, name of customer, or number
Personnel application forms	Name of applicant, or type of work (subject)
Purchase orders	Date, name of vendor, name of product, or number
Tax reports	Date, subject, or name of taxing body

Cross indexing is used when more than one subject is covered by the material or when several indicators are helpful in finding it. A report dealing with the subjects of market expansion and finances could be filed under the subject of markets, sales, future sales, finances, or costs. Cross indexes provide information as to where to place and to find the report;

however, numerous cross references should be avoided in order to simplify the work as much as possible. It is best to have these indexes on reference cards which can be maintained in a separate file. To find material on wages, the index card might read:

Wages	*See also* Compensation Fringe Benefits Job Evaluation Salary

This means that material on Wages may be found under all five terms. In the opinion of some, when an alphabetical arrangement is used, the cross-reference index should be by number or code. In contrast, when the numerical arrangement is followed, the cross index should be alphabetical.

Essential in most offices is a *basic classification index* which is a categorical grouping of subjects with appropriate detailed subheadings. In addition, *a relative index* is helpful since it shows, in a dictionary type listing, all possible words and combinations by which the material may be requested. All filing indexes should be kept current by making new entries for additional classifications as they occur. Main new sources will be key words, new terminology, or any other means by which material may be requested.

FILING PROCEDURE

For effective filing, a definite, well-planned filing procedure should be followed. The chief steps in such a procedure include the following:

1. *Checking release for filing.* Before any material is prepared for filing, it must first be checked to be sure it is released for filing. Material which is still being processed or referred to, or which, because of policy, is not retained by the company, should, of course, not be placed in the files.

2. *Reading and marking for filing.* Reading is done to determine the proper filing classification. A marking to indicate this classification can be shown by underscoring or circling a word or two on the paper or by stamping or writing the proper file data in the upper right corner. A colored pencil usually works very satisfactorily, as the contrast aids future reference. If there is a possibility of filing under several headings, it is helpful to consult the cross-reference index to insure use of the best classification for the material.

3. *Sorting.* To expedite filing, the material should be sorted by mark

showing the filing classification. Sorting can be performed entirely manually or with the use of a sorting device. In the former, the material is divided into neat piles on a table or desk, each pile being of a different classification. When this method is followed, it is best to sort all material according to major divisions, then each major division by subdivisions, and finally each subdivision as required. Figure 70 shows sorting devices

Courtesy: Erie Railroad, Cleveland

FIG. 70.   Sorting waybills in a large office. Approximately three million waybills per year are sorted in this office.

being used in a large office. The device consists of dividers properly indexed and hinged, at intervals of about ¼ inch up to 1 inch, to a common base section. Thus, a series of pockets is formed, and each item of the material to be sorted is dropped into the proper pocket. Different sizes are available, ranging from around 30 up to as many as 2,000 divisions or pockets.

4. *Filing material.* Each piece is filed under the proper classification, with the newest addition always on top or at the front of the contents in its respective folder. This actually amounts to dropping the material into the file at the right place.

5. *Charging material out.* A definite manner for handling the removal

of papers from the file is necessary in order to know where items are, in the event that several people want the papers at the same time, and also to minimize indiscriminate removals from the files. Records of charged-out materials can be handled in any one of four ways as illustrated by Figure 71: (*a*) by substitution card, (*b*) by out folder, (*c*) by out guide, or (*d*) by multiple charge-out form.

When the removed material is a single card or piece of paper, its place in the file can be occupied by a substitution card showing the name of the

FIG. 71. Media used in controlling charge-outs from filed material: (*a*) substitution card, (*b*) out folder, (*c*) out guide, and (*d*) multiple charge-out form.

person to whom the material is issued, along with the date and the initials of the file clerk issuing the material. Upon return of the material, the entries on the substitution card are lined out, and the card is reused. Out folders are ordinary file folders with one side printed for the recording of data concerning removals from that folder. The out guide is a pressboard guide with tab printed "Out" and a pocket or device to hold a single charge-out slip. It replaces a folder taken from the file and serves both as a record and as a marker for the borrowed material. When the withdrawn material is to be transferred from one user to another, a multiple charge-out form is used. As shown in Figure 71 the date, identification, and route of material are written on the multiple forms. One copy of this form is attached to the substitution card, out folder, or out guide. A second copy is filed in a tickler file for follow-up. Other copies are attached to the material so that, as each individual or department using the material finishes with it, a line is drawn through the name or department on the route list; the top copy is returned to the filing department; and the the remaining copies and material are forwarded to the next name on the route list. The returned copy received by the filing department is attached to the tickler file copy; thus, there is a record of who has the material, without clearance of the filed material each time through the filing department.

FILING PRACTICES

Certain filing practices have been found helpful, and adherence to them will probably bring best results. However, in certain individual cases, slight deviations might work out advantageously, depending upon the circumstances. A complete list of these filing practices is beyond the scope of this book, but the more important ones include the following:

1. Use a sufficient number of guides to help place and find the material quickly. This usually means a guide for each inch of filing.

2. File material *behind* the guides.

3. Use colored tabs and labels to increase identification.

4. Provide, with reference to correspondence files, individual folders when five or more papers have accumulated. Crowded miscellaneous folders usually show need for more breakdowns of the alphabet.

5. Arrange material in folders so that the latest is at the front.

6. File each name according to (*a*) surname, (*b*) given name or initial, (*c*) middle name or initial, and (*d*) title, if important to retain.

Alexander, Charles D. (Dr.)

7. File "nothing before something."

Carter
Carter, George
Carter, George L.

8. File alphabetical material in exact sequence of letters, *A* through *Z,* to the last letter of the last word.

M & A Stores, Inc.
Maag, Robert C.
MacArthur, Thomas P.
Mack, Henry
MacTavish, Sam W.
Maleski, Franck C.
McGuire, William F.
Mead-Carters Co.

9. Treat compound words as one word.

Cohen, Julius I.
Co-operative Sales
Co-workers Order of Bart
Cutter, Frederick J.

10. Spell out abbreviated names.

Safety Tool and Tire Company
Saint Louis Poultry and Egg Company
Saint Paul Club
Salk, Meyer L.
Street, Theodore P.

11. Spell out numerals and abbreviations.

First National Bank
Three Thirty-Three Lake Building
Young Women's Christian Association

12. When names are identical, file by city; then state; and if necessary, by street address in city.

Carson, John M.
　Bangor, Maine
Carson, John M.
　Springfield, Mass.
Carson, John M.
　3719 Lyndale Road
　Springfield, Ohio
Carson, John M.
　5127 Western Street
　Springfield, Ohio

13. To save time with alphabetic material, sort by first segregating into four groups, such as A–F, G–L, M–R, and S–Z; then, sort each group according to the first letter. For numeric material, first sort 0–2, 3–5, and 6–9; then sort each group by the first digit.

14. Transfer material to inactive file regularly and at stated intervals.[4]

FILING CABINETS

Filing cabinets are available in many different sizes and types, but those for cards—3 x 5 inch or 5 x 8 inch—letter, and legal-size papers are most popular. The equipment is available in sizes from one to six drawers. The one- and two-drawer models are used on a desk or table; the three-drawer is desk height and is usually used beside a desk, providing ready accessibility to papers frequently used. Four-drawer models are used for counter purposes. The five- and six-drawer files provide extra filing capacities for the floor space occupied. A standard file drawer holds about 5,000 sheets of paper, 300 file folders, and 26 file guides.

The mechanical details of files differ with the manufacturers. Most files feature a ball-bearing, full progressive sidearm suspension which provides smooth rolling action of the drawer and permits easy opening and closing. A sliding, adjustable device known as a "follower" holds the papers upright in the drawer. It can be pulled up tight and snapped or locked in position; a slight force releases the device and permits it to be moved to another position. In some models the material is placed in hanging or suspending folders which transfer the weight from the drawer bottom to two top rails on either side, running the length of the drawer. Suspended folders provide fingertip ease of filing and the folders cannot slump. The equipment is available with or without locks, insulated for fire protection, and in several colors and finishes to harmonize with the color scheme of the office.

SIDE-FILING OR LATERAL CABINETS

Proponents of this type of filing cabinet stress the ease of getting to all filed material, the fast handling of filing work—25 percent more than that with other types, and savings in floor space—about 50 percent compared with a regular four-drawer based on filing inches per square foot of floor area. Lateral filing cabinets can be divided into four groups: (1) drawer, (2) box, (3) shelf type, and (4) suspension. The first is similar to a

---

[4] Transfer of filed material is discussed in the following chapter on records retention.

regular end-opening filing cabinet, but in the side-file the drawer opens from the side. These units can be equipped to handle either regular or suspension folders. All material can be reached easily. The second, or box, consists of top and side open-edged metal boxes or trays hooked onto the rails of a freestanding metal frame, which is assembled without nuts, bolts, or screws. The frame is tailored to fit individual needs and the boxes, into which the material is placed, hang at a slight angle, creating a stair-step effect to expedite the filing work. Top- or side-tab folders can be used. Figure 72 shows the detail of this type filing. The third, or shelf

Courtesy: Tab Products Co., San Francisco

FIG. 72.   Detail of the cutaway box permitting working folder corners. The box type is for records not requiring closed storage.

type, features compartments of filed material exposed for ready accessibility, as shown by Figure 73. Folders can be slid out instead of lifted out, separators within compartments can be supplied if desired, and open file doors serve as work surfaces. In the fourth, or suspension, filed material is contained in special folders suspended from a pair of rods. The folders, provided with labels at front edge, are available in many different sizes to accommodate different sizes and weights to be filed. Figure 74 shows an efficient filing of computer tabulating sheets and supplies and a detail of the file.

Within this category of side filing, modification of the shelf and the suspension types give rise to the so-called open-shelf type of filing equipment. This has won wide approval for many odd-sized items such as

Courtesy: Tab Products Co., San Francisco

FIG. 73.   Shelf-type steel filing cabinets with retractable doors.

FIG. 74.   (Above) Suspension filing being used for computer tab forms. (Right) Detail of file construction.

Courtesy: Robert P. Gillette Co., Inc., Columbia, S.C.

magnetic reels, paper tapes, artwork, photographs, and line drawings. The units are adjustable with regard to their own size as well as to the space for filed materials, will therefore handle both large and small sizes of materials, and are priced satisfactorily.

RECIPROCATING FILES

The employee can either go to the work, or the work can be brought to the employee. This latter situation is stressed in reciprocating file equipment. By its use the employee can remain seated with necessary machines and tools located within easy reach, and the file can be moved forward and backward as required. Use of this type of file (1) reduces employee fatigue, (2) eliminates travel time, (3) minimizes waiting time at files, and (4) allows full supervision, since all equipment is at desk-level height and under full view of the supervisor.

ROTARY FILES

This name applies to filing cabinets mounted on a platform which revolves or to filing cabinets in which the filed material is held to the periphery of a wheel which revolves, thus affording a ready and quick locating means at writing height. In the former type, the arrangement is designed to expedite work methods. It frequently makes one large set of records quickly available to several employees with work stations around the edge of the common file. It can be thought of as a reciprocating file with a circular pattern. (See top view of Figure 75.) In the second type, posting is convenient without removal of the filed material. This wheel-type unit provides speedy handling—large motion savings up to 75 percent have been estimated—and compactness. The range of sizes is from small units about the size of a telephone to large units approximately 36 inches high. The capacity varies, of course, with the size of the wheel; for example, a unit having a 21-inch-diameter wheel, handling 5 x 8-inch cards, has a capacity of 6,000 cards. In most cases the filed cards have punched openings at bottom to provide a gripping effect to a retaining rod, but units are available which hold nonpunched cards, folders, photographs, and drawings. Both single- and multiwheel units are offered, as well as a special mechanism for stabilizing the rotation. A four-unit model is shown in bottom view of Figure 75.

MOTORIZED CARD FILES

When the work requires access to a large number of filed cards, a motorized card file may be useful. It is electrically operated and brings in a few seconds any desired tray of cards in the unit at convenient writing

Courtesy: Acme Visible Records, Inc., Crozet, Va.

Courtesy: Wheeldex and Simpla Products, Inc., White Plains, N.Y.

FIG. 75. (*Top*) Six clerks have immediate access to 60,000 customer account records in this rotary file. (*Bottom*) A multiwheel unit of rotary file equipment.

height to a seated operator. The cards are filed vertically, and the trays are removable. Units are available in various card sizes and capacities. Savings in time and effort result from the use of motorized card files. Demanding specifications in respect to space limitations, floor layout, and operational problems can be met. A motorized card file unit is shown in Figure 76.

Courtesy: Remington Rand, Inc., New York

FIG. 76. A motorized card file providing an ideal work station with availability to a large number of cards.

VISIBLE FILES—CARDS HORIZONTAL

The name "visible file" reveals its outstanding feature, namely, providing for the user, at a glance, visible information in the file. Probably the most common and the one we shall discuss first is the type with the cards filed horizontally; however, it is not the only style as we shall later see. The cards are filed horizontally in a shallow slide or tray in such a manner that the bottom margin of each card is exposed, providing for quick visibility. In this margin are pertinent data concerning the information on the major area of the card. Varying widths of margin exposure may be used; standard equipment provides $\frac{3}{16}$-inch to $\frac{5}{16}$-inch margin visibility. Card capacity per tray depends upon the card size and the margin exposure used, but 80 cards per tray is a good average figure. Units are available with different numbers of trays. Each card is fastened in such a way that it can be raised and flipped by pivoting about the top edge. Thus, the complete information on any card can be viewed in full, or

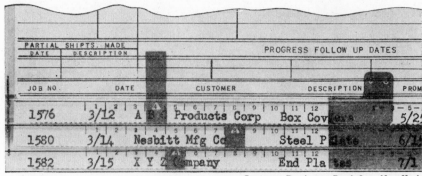

Courtesy: Remington Rand, Inc., New York

FIG. 77. An effective follow-up signaling system. On the top card, the signal over the 4 indicates April, the month in which follow-up should be made. The signal at the right of the card at the 3 indicates the day of the month on which the follow-up is due.

additional data can be written on the card with the tray used as an armrest.

In some equipment, the top edge of the card is fastened directly onto the tray; while in other equipment, "pockets" made of strong kraft paper are fastened directly onto the tray and the card is held in place by inserting the bottom edge into a flap made by a U-shaped plastic strip at the bottom of the pocket. The top of the card is held by inserting the corners into slots precut in the pocket.

Effective signaling to denote certain information on the card is one of the outstanding features of visible filing equipment using cards filed horizontally. By sliding different-colored plastic markers along the visible margins, definite dates or quantities, which are signals for specific actions, are brought out in bold relief. By such signals, a whole tray of cards can be scanned and the items requiring immediate attention quickly spotted. Figure 77 illustrates a signaling system for accurate follow-up.

Both manual and electrical visible file units are available. The electric unit eliminates stooping, reaching, pulling out trays, writing at inconvenient levels, and pushing back trays. It excludes many causes of operator fatigue, raises productivity, and saves floor space. One popular unit holds 60 trays, counterbalanced in two equal banks which travel up and down when the unit is actuated. Figure 78 shows illustrations of the visible file operated manually and also the unit operated electrically.

Visible card file equipment is also in book form. Approximately 2,000 cards can be kept in one binder. The book form affords portability and a posting surface always at desk height. Binders are made to lie perfectly flat when open, to lock against any possible accidental shifting of record sequence, and to lift and guide sheets into proper position when the binder is closed.

VISIBLE FILES—CARDS VERTICALLY

Another type of visible file is that designed for use where cards are filed vertically. With this style, common card sizes are from about 3 to 20 inches in width and 5 to 12 inches in height. They are similar in appearance to the printed forms for machine- and hand-posting work. Two types will be discussed here: (1) the magnetic card and (2) the shingled, clipped-corner card.

In the magnetic-card visible file, the records are instantly visible and accessible. They are not fastened in any way to the tray, making rearrangement, removal, or addition of cards to the file a very simple task. Very thin metal strips are included in the cards during manufacture. The unit is powered by magnetic force and operates on the basis of the repellent force of magnets separating one card from the next at any point of reference. A batch of 15 to 20 cards can be fanned out quickly with just a touch of the fingertips, and information on these cards can be read very easily. Figure 79 illustrates this type file.

In the shingled clipped-corner card file, one or both of the upper corners of the card are cut away in order to provide diagonal indexing margins; in addition, the horizontal and one of the vertical margins of the card are used for indexing. Cards are placed in the file in an offset arrangement, so that the top, diagonal, and side margins of the card are exposed or visible. The card is held in position by means of a notched arrangement at the bottom of the card which fits into a receiving device at the bottom of the file, and the design is such that cards can easily be inserted or removed. Both sides of the card can be used, and signaling devices similar to those already discussed can be employed. Figure 80 shows the arrangement of cards in the file. With this equipment, the finding time is minimized,

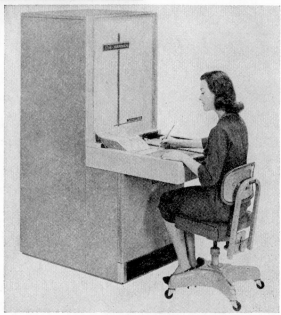

Courtesy: Remington Rand, Inc., New York

FIG. 78. Visible file equipment where cards are filed horizontally. On the top is the manually operated unit with tray withdrawn and ready for posting. On the bottom is the electrically operated unit. The operator presses one of several bars in front of her, causing the desired tray to come out of the unit at writing height in a matter of seconds.

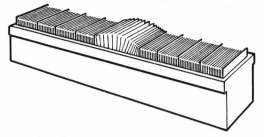

FIG. 79. Side view of magnetic-card visible file. A batch of cards can be fanned out to permit visibility and ease of finding card information.

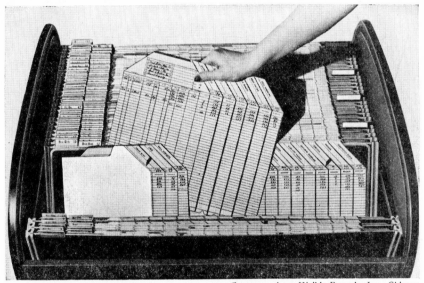

Courtesy: Acme Visible Records, Inc., Chicago

FIG. 80. The arrangement of cards in a file. Groups of cards can be removed and replaced just as easily as one card. This is commonly called an open tub file.

thumbing through cards is eliminated, and exceedingly quick scanning over large numbers of cards is possible—for example, nearly 7,000 cards, 10 x 5 inches in size, can be accommodated in one file unit.

FILED STRIPS

Another type of file is the so-called filed strips used when quick reference to records containing a small quantity of data is needed. It is useful for maintaining lists which undergo changes, such as names and addresses of customers, prices, rates, bin locations, directories, reservations, hospital indexes, telephone and switchboard data, and routings.

Either of two methods can be followed. The first consists of (1) typing or otherwise writing the data on scored and special sheet material, which is made of resilient veneer covered on both sides with paper; (2) separating the sections by breaking along the scored line; and (3) placing the strips in a frame by bending them slightly and snapping the ends under the side channels of the frame. The second method consists of writing the data on small die-cut cards which snap or button on a holding frame. This places the cards in an offset arrangement with the upper margin of the card plainly visible. With either method, the frames can be suspended on desk stands, wall brackets, and rotaries. Figure 81 shows

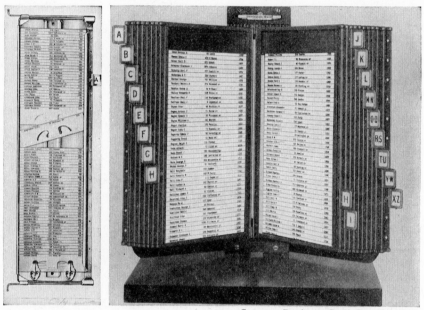

Courtesy: Remington Rand, Inc., New York

FIG. 81. Two types of visible reference record equipment used where the amount of data is small and where fast, frequent reference is required.

illustrations of this equipment. To indicate special conditions applying to a particular name, a signaling device of a shape and color code is either slid over, or attached to, a record. Different-colored strips and cards are also available and can be used for signaling purposes, if desired.

MANAGERIAL ORGANIZING AND FILING WORK

From the viewpoint of organizing, filing commonly is on a decentralized basis, which provides accessibility for those needing the files, flexibility in arrangement, and reasonably satisfactory service. However, too frequently there is no one person with fixed responsibility for the over-all planning and coordinating of filing activities. One person in charge of all filing helps promote needed study and improvements in filing. Perhaps an arrangement centralized from the viewpoint of managerial operation and decentralized as to the physical location of files is superior. With centralized management authority, the best of filing knowledge and practices from the over-all company viewpoint can be put into use. However, the exact organizational plan depends upon individual requirements and understanding them. Filing needs differ. The type of material, the work habits of the employees using the files, the normal filing usage, the flow of work, frequency of records, and information required are several of the more influential considerations.

MOTIVATING FILING PERSONNEL

Better placement of personnel for filing work is needed. In too many instances, the attitude prevails that the untrained office employee who cannot be fitted in elsewhere because of lack of some office skill should be given filing work. Entirely overlooked is the fundamental truth that filing personnel should possess certain attributes, including a sense of orderliness, accuracy, manual dexterity, quick reading comprehension, and a liking for detail.

Emphasize a realistic approach consisting of these four facets. First, with the assistance of the filing personnel, secure suitable filing equipment and adopt practices to fit the needs of the enterprise. Second, establish what can reasonably be expected from the filing personnel. For example, are all requests clear and complete? Frequently, the file clerk is expected to have an ability to find a piece of paper even though she has never seen it and does not know what it was about, who it was from, or when it was written. Third, make sincere efforts to upgrade filing. All key and office personnel should be made aware of the importance of filing and of the helpful contributions of those performing this work. Fourth, adjust wages of the filing personnel. Of the total cost for filing, most is for labor, and filing can never be more efficient than the people doing the filing.

THE CONTROLLING OF FILING

Standards for filing equipment, supplies, handling, and indexing should be developed and followed. With these as a guide, along with periodic follow-ups, the manager can determine whether standards are being followed and whether the level of filing work is satisfactory. Spot checks for accuracy are advisable. For this purpose a committee can be used in order to generate more interest in filing and enhance an awareness of needed improvements. Standards will vary among different companies due to the type of records and the working conditions. However, to give an idea of what can be done, the following expectancies are shown, based on data from a number of companies:

Task	Units per Hour
Sorting letters and filing alphabetically	180
Filing 5 x 8-inch cards in an alphabetical vertical file	315
Locating and pulling letters from an alphabetical file	110
Filing vouchers numerically	700
Marking one-page letters for filing	220

The existence of duplicate files is a major problem. Adequate controls to minimize the following causes must be enforced: (1) misunderstanding and failure to specify where office files will be located and maintained, (2) lack of determining the number of copies to be filed by particular records or documents, and (3) failure to curb a tendency by management members to create and keep papers for every contingency. It helps to place files in locations convenient to those frequently using them in order to reduce the number of duplicate files.

Cost can be used in file controlling, but its use is not extensive. Some over-all cost constraints usually are helpful and should be established. Of the total cost of filing, equipment represents about 12–14 percent, floor space about 10–12 percent, and labor about 70–75 percent. The conclusion is inescapable. Filing labor is vital. Filing requires sizable expenditures. The cost of filing using a four-drawer correspondence file is about $225 per year. Thirty files therefore mean $6,750 annual cost. Substantiating data for one file cabinet per year follow:

Rent for 5½ sq.ft. per cabinet and aisle at $2.00 per sq.ft.	$ 11.00
Depreciation on cabinet	7.00
Transfer cases	8.00
Labor	165.00
File guides and folders	10.00
Overhead and supervision	18.00
Miscellaneous	4.00
Total	$223.00

Cost data to shed light on the most suitable equipment should be sought. Surplus equipment can be transferred from one area to another, and, to control purchases, a careful review of all requests for additional equipment should be adopted.

CHAPTER EIGHT

RECORDS RETENTION

The truth is, one's vocation is never some far-off possibility.
It is always the simple round of duties which the passing hours bring.
—John W. Dulles

THE CREATING and filing of a large volume of records and papers establishes a need for the disposition of all files as soon as they no longer serve any useful purpose. Unless periodic culling of files takes place, there is a staggering amount of file space taken up by routine papers such as outdated correspondence, acknowledgements, inventory records, first drafts of reports, and memoranda. Their presence in the file clutter up the entire contents and make it more difficult to locate important and useful papers as the demand for them arises. You cannot file and forget.

All records go through three different stages: (1) active use—quick access is important, (2) storage—for possible use, and (3) elimination—no longer of use. Recognition of these three basic steps, and of the needless expense incurred by not properly managing this life cycle of all records, suggests actions designed to keep worthless materials out of files, periodically review filed materials to eliminate what is no longer necessary, store certain records in a storage area for possible future use, and preserve only those having permanent value to the enterprise. This is the essential makeup of records retention.

MEANING OF RECORDS RETENTION

Records retention deals with the disposition of records and concerns storing those that must be retained and destroying those that are or become worthless. Records retention is an essential part of records management and must be coordinated with that of other office management activities, so that the necessary paper work is done at lowest cost and yet provides maximum service. The activities of a sound records retention program include provisions to:

1. Establish a tight schedule of retention periods for every type of record and all its copies.

2. Remove from active files all materials that should be retained temporarily but are not needed for current operations, employing well-timed and orderly procedures for this work.

3. Destroy obsolete records.

4. Establish and maintain a convenient, safe, and low-cost area for record storage and index the exact location of each type of record.

5. Take charge of all microfilming of records to insure that only necessary copies are made.

6. Show facts on volume and cost of records management and, if necessary, revise activities for greater effectiveness and service.

7. Participate in purchasing decisions for new filing equipment and supplies.

ADVANTAGES OF RECORDS-RETENTION PROGRAM

Such a program can be quite extensive. It requires good management, foresight, judgment, and especially a steadfastness of purpose. The rewards, however, are high. Better filing efficiency is gained since inactive material is removed, thus reducing finding time. Space savings are also achieved—throwing out records that have become useless means less space is needed. Also, storing useful but inactive records in an inexpensive storage area means dollar savings. And avoidance from accidental or premature destruction of records is assured. Furthermore, the retained records are better protected and safeguarded. Equipment designed especially for storage can be utilized, and the records are not subject to possible mutilation as a result of frequent handling.

Typically about 58 percent of all filed material is eliminated, 16 percent placed in records storage, and the balance, 26 percent, remains in the office area as active material. Think of it. Only one paper in four remains in the office files. The savings in finding time and space are tremendous. The National Records Management Council, Inc., a nonprofit organization, estimates only 5 percent of all records filed are ever referred to after a year and 5 percent of the references made deal with records over five years old. A large public utility reported to be spending nearly $24 million to maintain some 200,000 filing cabinets, adopted a records retention program and trimmed this cost to $17 million and with better service and efficiency. The gains by several other companies are shown by Figure 82.

WITHOUT RECORDS RETENTION
PROGRAM

WITH RECORDS RETENTION
PROGRAM

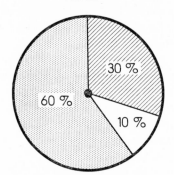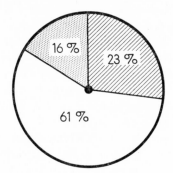

30 percent retained in active files
60 percent retained in inactive files
10 percent destroyed

23 percent retained in active files
16 percent retained in inactive files
61 percent destroyed

FIG. 82. Typical disposition of records by companies without and those with records-retention programs.

STEPS IN RECORDS-RETENTION PROGRAM

The objective of a records-retention program is to retain only needed records only as long as they are needed. To this end the program provides a smooth flow of records from the office to storage and eventually to destruction. Such a program requires four steps, made up of these actions: (1) take inventory of records, (2) determine record retention periods, (3) provide effective storage facilities, and (4) transfer the records. These steps are not difficult, but they must be carried out faithfully and carefully to insure success of the program.

TAKE INVENTORY OF RECORDS

Each company should strive to develop its own records retention based on an analysis of the actual use made of its own records. To copy what another company has decided frequently results in serious shortcomings. The analysis might begin with a cursory review of the entire enterprise to obtain background and understanding of the current work and to spot what records are used and what ones are filed for satisfactory operation. Following this, a survey is in order to determine (1) what is filed; (2) how much is filed—its size and quantity; (3) where it is filed—including the copies, if any; (4) how often it was used during specific preceding periods; (5) when, if ever, it is permanently removed from file; and (6) what is done with permanently removed material. In some instances, this inventory work is expedited by classifying the material by type or by department. Information applicable to several departments can be studied as a group, thus relating the types of information common to the several units. Usually a simple form is used upon which to record the data.

From the survey data, the value of each record is weighed. Questions decided are: Should this record be filed at all? How long should this record remain in the file? Is it advisable to retain this record in storage? Particular attention is paid to records presently having long-term retention. Experience shows that many retention times can be cut measurably below the periods formerly believed necessary.

DETERMINE RECORD-RETENTION PERIODS

Most offices are confronted with the problem of how long to retain active and inactive file material. The answer lies in knowing what to save and how to store it. This, in turn, depends primarily upon the usefulness of the material to managers, and the legal requirements. The period of retention differs among companies, but there is a tendency toward the development of standard practices.

Group decision making is advisable to determine what papers to retain and for how long a period. Usually, the controller, the legal counsel, the tax counsel, and the manager of records retention should be included in this group; they can decide basic issues essential to the program. For the most part, this group sets forth policy instructions on which operating decisions can be based by the manager of records retention.

Papers that are essential to the company's security should be kept. Proof of assets and liabilities is important. Papers giving proof of ownership, property, inventories, machinery, and buildings are included in this category. Insurance is recovered on proof, not guesswork. Records dealing with transactions should be saved. These include receipt of money, proof of payment, proof of expenses or purchases, and payroll. Also, documents providing proof of usage should be retained, for they are vital in matters dealing with research, engineering, and patents. If the company becomes involved in infringement or other patent-suit claims, certain drawings, properly coded, numbered, and preserved, form the basis for prosecution or defense. Historical data of various types often prove valuable in that they provide trends and statistical analysis helpful in the company's planning efforts. Such data should be retained if there is a reasonable possibility that they will be used in the future or will be referred to for improving decision making by relating the reasons given *why* certain decisions were made in the past with the outcome of such decisions.

Figure 83 shows selected retention periods for various records. These values represent the consensus of authorities on record storage and reflect current thinking in this area. However, the statute of limitations, which varies for different documents among states, regulatory activities by government agencies, and personal preferences should be considered in the choice. The statute of limitations specifies the length of time a record is alive according to law. Figure 84 shows these periods by specific documents, by states.

Accounts receivable	10	Insurance—property	8
Agreements with employees	P*	Labor clock records	5
Annual and monthly reports	P	Labor earnings records	P
Articles of incorporation	P	Medical histories	P
Attendance records of employees	7	Minute book of directors meeting	P
Bids	3	Paid bills	8
Cash books	P	Patent records	P
Charge slips	10	Registered mail	5
Checks canceled	10	Requisitions	3
Correspondence—		Sales expenses	6
credit and collection	7	Shipping tickets	6
—purchase	5	Tax bills and statements	P
Delivery receipts	3	Time and motion studies	P
Dividend checks	10	Union labor contracts	P
Financial statements	P	Wage rates	8
General ledger	P		

*P = Permanent

FIG. 83. Suggested schedule for retention of various records in years.

Based on the information obtained from the inventory of records, suggested retention periods, and judgment, records of varying importance can be classified as to their retention. For convenience, they can be divided into four groups:

1. *Nonessential.* Records so classified should never be filed. Since they have value for a short period only—perhaps a few seconds—retaining them is wasteful. Included are pencil notations, routine inquiries, and announcements.

2. *Helpful.* Records in this group can assist, but only for a very limited time, perhaps four to five weeks. After this period, their usefulness is completed. If filed, they should be placed in a separate drawer or cabinet and destroyed as their helpfulness ceases. An example is general correspondence, most of which has a useful life of not over four weeks.

3. *Important.* These include records containing information of value for relatively long periods—up to five or six years. They should first be filed in the office for handy reference; but ultimately, as they lose their current usefulness, they should be transferred to storage. How long they remain in the office depends upon the type of record and the retention period established. Many firms keep records such as invoices, accounts

STATE	OPEN ACCOUNTS	CONTRACTS IN WRITING	
		Under Seal	Not under Seal
Alabama......................	3	10	6
Alaska.......................	5	6	6
Arizona......................	3	6	6
Arkansas.....................	3	5	5
California....................	varies	4	4
Colorado.....................	6	6	6
Connecticut..................	6	17	6
Delaware.....................	3	20	3
District of Columbia...........	3	12	3
Florida......................	3	20	5
Hawaii......................	varies	4	4
Georgia.....................	4	20	6
Idaho.......................	4	5	5
Illinois......................	5	10	varies
Indiana.....................	6	20	10
Iowa........................	5	10	10
Kansas......................	3	5	5
Kentucky....................	5	15	15
Louisiana....................	varies	varies	varies
Maine.......................	6	20	6
Maryland....................	3	12	3
Massachusetts................	6	20	6
Michigan....................	6	6	6
Minnesota...................	6	6	6
Mississippi..................	3	6	6
Missouri....................	5	10	10
Montana....................	5	8	8
Nebraska....................	4	5	5
Nevada......................	4	6	6
New Hampshire...............	6	20	6
New Jersey...................	6	16	6
New Mexico..................	4	6	6
New York....................	6	6	6
North Carolina...............	3	10	3
North Dakota.................	6	6	6
Ohio........................	6	15	15
Oklahoma....................	3	5	5
Oregon......................	6	10	6
Pennsylvania.................	6	20	6
Rhode Island.................	6	20	6
South Carolina...............	6	20	6
South Dakota.................	6	20	6
Tennessee...................	6	6	6
Texas.......................	2	4	4
Utah........................	4	8	6
Vermont.....................	6	varies	6
Virginia.....................	3	10	5
Washington..................	3	6	6
West Virginia................	5	10	10
Wisconsin...................	6	varies	6
Wyoming....................	8	10	10

FIG. 84.   Statutes of limitations, in years, for specified documents.

receivable, sales records, quotations, and financial statements in active files for one to two years, then transfer to storage.

4. *Vital.* As the name implies, these records are paramount. They are retained permanently. They may be transferred to the storage area after a given period of time, but they are never destroyed. Vital records include legal papers of incorporation, titles to ownership, deeds, and reports to stockholders.

PROVIDE A GOOD STORAGE AREA

A clean, dry area should be designated for records retention. Proper conditions of temperature, circulation of air, and humidity should be provided. Traditionally, storage rooms have been the attics of business; they should be regarded as attractive work areas. The floor area must withstand a relatively high weight, as much as 250 pounds per square foot. Location can be either (1) on-site (same as office) or (2) off-site (away from office).

Various types of equipment can be used for storing records. The following are of special interest: (1) specially designed fiberboard drawer files and (2) storage boxes on shelving. A specially designed fiberboard drawer file combines the drawer, shelving, and base, all in one unit. A steel framework carries the entire weight load. The drawer files are interlocking, as illustrated by the right picture of Figure 85. The drawers are locked together solidly, each locking to the one below and the one above it. The unit "builds its own steel framework as you stack it." As many as 20 drawers can be stacked in one tier. There is no buckling, sagging, or warping. Different sizes are available for punched cards, letter, and legal-size papers. The total space is devoted to drawer units, which results in a compact, efficient use of storage space giving the high storage ratio of 8 to 1, i.e., the cubic feet of records to square feet of floor space. For bulk storage where reference is infrequent, larger containers with the same interlocking feature can be used. Each container is about 15 inches by 24 inches and holds two boxes, one of which can be used for letter, the other for legal size as shown by Figure 86.

Storage boxes on ordinary shelving are also used. They afford maximum economy in dead records storage. The boxes are built of high-test corrugated fiberboard especially designed to withstand rough usage and to prevent mildew and damage from dirt or moisture. A variety of sizes is supplied so that the stored material fits snugly in the box. The shelving is assembled quickly without tools and can be extended by adding extensional units. The shelving can be dismantled and reassembled in a new location in a matter of minutes.

Courtesy: Bankers Box Co., Franklin Park, Ill.

FIG. 85.   Interlocking fiberboard drawer files form a compact and sub-stantial storage file.

For records in storage, a system of indexing should be adopted, so that all such material can be located quickly. The information can be kept on small index cards or on sheets in a loose-leaf notebook. It should include subject classification, shelf number, box number or name, and scheduled date for ultimate destruction. If is important that each container be labeled plainly.

At least once a year, a list should be prepared showing what stored original records should be destroyed. It can be compiled readily from data on the index cards. This list is then submitted to the office manager or designated executive for approval and authority to proceed. When this has been granted, the material is destroyed and the list filed permanently for future reference.

TRANSFER RECORDS

The transfer of records as a part of a records-retention program really starts before the material is filed, in that only material considered to have future worth or value should be filed. Keeping worthless materials out of

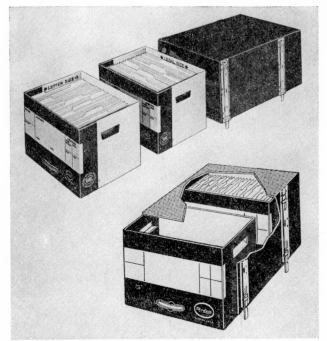

Courtesy: Bankers Box Co., Franklin Park, Ill.

FIG. 86. Both storage boxes slide into the stacking shell. This tandem arrangement provides maximum storage in minimum space.

the files is easier and more realistic than getting worthless materials removed once they are filed.

The systematic transfer of records implements the records-retention program. Several moves are necessary, including transfer from active to inactive files and from inactive files to storage area. In each case the transfer may also lead to a decision for their destruction should the records at that stage be considered worthless. Reference to Figure 87 is helpful in discussing the various transfers.

As previously stated, material classified as nonessential should never be filed, but should be destroyed immediately. "Helpful" material is filed in a separate file for the limited period, then destroyed. Material considered important or vital is filed (step No. 1) and subsequently transferred to the inactive file as a normal practice (step No. 2). Material cannot remain in the files indefinitely—the physical space becomes exhausted. As indicated in the figure with a four-drawer filing cabinet, the top drawers can be used

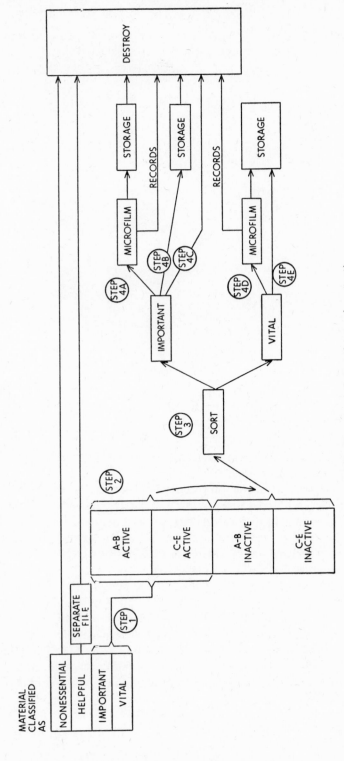

FIG. 87. A program of records retention.

for current material and the bottom two for inactive material. This arrangement affords convenient reference to inactive material, necessary from time to time in every office. When the five-drawer file is used, a common arrangement to follow is illustrated by Figure 88.

The transferring of material can be done in one of two main ways: (1) the entire unit, or periodically; and (2) the individual, or perpetually. The former requires that all material be transferred at a scheduled time. Usually, an annual basis is used—at the beginning of the calendar year, fiscal year, or busy season. The material remains in the original folders

1 INACTIVE	3 INACTIVE	6 INACTIVE	8 INACTIVE
1	4	6	9
2	5	7	10
3	4 INACTIVE	8	9 INACTIVE
2 INACTIVE	5 INACTIVE	7 INACTIVE	10 INACTIVE

FIG. 88.   Arrangement for active and inactive material in five-drawer files.

and is moved bodily. New folders are used for the new material in the current file. The individual, or perpetual, places time limits on individual papers by appropriate marks on the folders. Then, periodically, at intervals of about two or three months—or perpetually, at irregular intervals—the files are screened, and papers found to have been in the file past the allowable limit are transferred to the inactive file. In cases where the transaction is terminated, i.e., a settlement granted or a sale closed, the material is transferred immediately, regardless of date.

From the inactive files all materials are removed periodically and sorted (step No. 3 of Figure 87). The material in these files is either important or vital material. The former is handled in three different ways: microfilmed, records destroyed, films placed in storage, and ultimately destroyed (step 4A); records placed in storage and eventually destroyed (step 4B); or records destroyed, having outlived their span of importance (step 4*C*).[1] If the material is classified as vital, step 4*D*, consisting of microfilming, destroying records, and placing films in storage, can be followed; or step 4*E*, placing the material in storage, can be adopted.

This program may vary somewhat in individual applications. For example, microfilm may not be used at all, or it may be found more practical to eliminate step No. 3 (sorting), microfilm all records, and use the microfilms for reference in all cases.

If records are placed in storage, many records managers suggest marking the destruction date on the material at the time of its transfer to storage. This may be a date stamped on the material or a notice to destroy in "one year," "two years," or "retain permanently." In any event, as stated above, all transferred material should be classified, properly labeled, and indexed so that it can be found if needed.

MICROFILMING

"Microfilming" is a photographic means of retaining the information given in office papers. The materials are first photographed on film at reduced sizes; then, the film is developed, to serve as the permanent record. Figure 89 shows several popular arrangements in microfilming material and a modern microfilming machine.

One of the first commercial applications of microfilming was in banks, where it was used in connection with checks. The list of applications grew steadily, and microfilming is now associated with many types of paper materials. It is an accepted part of many records-retention programs. One interesting application is to mount a single microfilm frame into a punched card which carries identifying and classifying data of the microfilmed subject which can be a large engineering drawing, specifications, or photograph. It is an easy matter to store and sort the punched cards, giving quick, accurate handling to what otherwise is a clumsy, time-consuming task.

Microfilming is available to the small as well as to the large enterprise. Outside concerns specializing in microfilming work will microfilm records either in the office of the company or in their own plant. The cost for this service, including film and developing, varies from $4 to $6 for each 1,000 pieces, depending upon the size and quantity of the material, whether hand or automatic feed can be used, and whether one or two sides are to be microfilmed.

The use of microfilming effects a great saving of storage space. About 98–99 percent of storage space can be saved, since one to two file cabinets of film hold the equivalent of a hundred cabinets of original records. In

---

[1] Microfilming is discussed immediately below.

A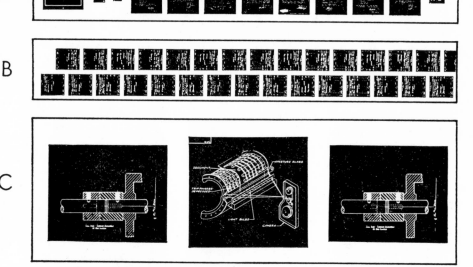

B

C

Courtesy: Burroughs Corp., Detroit

FIG. 89. *Top, A:* For standard size letters, 16-mm. film and 17-to-1 reduction are popular. *Top, B:* For infrequent reference, a double line—one for front, the other for back of the document, 23-to-1 reduction, is recommended. *Top, C:* For engineering drawings and ledger sheets, a 17-to-1 reduction and 25-mm. film are used. *Bottom:* One compact machine handles all microfilming needs, including high-fidelity filming to high-clarity reading.

addition, the chances of losing a document are minimized. The photographs on the film are in sequence like links of a chain; once a paper is photographed, there is no danger of the photograph being lost unless the whole roll of microfilm is lost. Furthermore, with microfilm, the retained materials are clean and easily handled; and they reduce the fire hazard, because the film is of the acetate, noncombustible type.

On the other hand, microfilming has its drawbacks. The courts usually prefer original documents, but will accept microfilmed material when failure to produce the original is adequately explained. Usually, microfilming must be established as a regular procedure and one not motivated by any suspicion of fraud. Microfilming may tend to retain temporarily an excess of records because it is easier to microfilm all records and file the films than it is to decide what materials have future use and microfilm them only. Also the use of microfilming requires special equipment; a viewer is the minimum requirement. Furthermore, employees must be trained for the specialized techniques required, and these skills are somewhat different from those required for most office work.

HEAD OF RECORDS-RETENTION PROGRAM

In most cases, it is best to have one person in charge of a records-retention program. The person should have adequate authority to direct and maintain the program. To a great extent, the success of the program is determined by the caliber of person heading the unit and the relationship of the records-retention unit to the other office units. Preferably, this head should report to an executive in a high enough organizational level to get top management support and opinions.

Committees should be used to assist the designated head of the records-retention work. As stated earlier in this chapter, a committee to establish policies and decide retention periods for each type of paper is effective, but putting into action and managing the program is better vested in a competent individual. Consultation with department heads is in order because they usually are well qualified to suggest which of their own records probably should be retained and for how long a period.

INSTILL CONFIDENCE IN RECORDS RETENTION

The manager of records retention must instill a feeling of confidence in the records-retention activities and results. All office personnel, as well as key management people, must believe in the accuracy, completeness, and usefulness of the field material. Unless they do, they are quite likely to keep important records in their own desks or special files rather than trust them with records retention.

This development of a favorable attitude toward the records-retention program is important. If a minimum number of temporary and permanent files is wanted the personnel dealing with filing and retaining records must have a reasonably responsible frame of mind toward this objective. Employees need to know the managers' mood toward having lean, thin files and then govern themselves accordingly. Normally, filing employees can not be expected to evaluate the future relevance of various papers. Without explicit instructions or some knowledge of what is customarily retained, they are quite likely to place in the files what seems important now. And in these efforts, they understandably err on the side of safety— it is better to have a document than not have it. Fewer complaints are voiced by managers about buying filing equipment and supplies than on learning that a needed document has been destroyed. Then too, discontinuing the practice of filing nearly every paper does not come easily. Filing of "certain papers" may continue—just in case. There is a certain reluctance not to file copies of replies to such correspondence as invitations to branch office openings, congratulatory notes, and letters of introduction and instead to pencil a notation on the original letter that a reply was made. Rough drafts of speeches, articles, improvement lists, and the like so easily are placed in the files. And these acts are taken by personnel who honestly feel they are doing "what is best."

A manual supplying information on the procedures and practices of the records-retention group is also helpful. Data on the type of material stored, the indexing system, retention schedule, and specific duties of records-retention personnel should be clearly written and made available to anyone whose work is affected by records retention. Such a manual is extremely beneficial for obtaining better understanding and for training new employees in records-retention work.

CONTROLLING AND RECORDS RETENTION

An effective means of control is to limit the quantity of records per employee. The amount permitted will depend upon the type of business operation. In public utilities, for example, an amount of 5 cubic feet of records per employee on payroll is considered satisfactory. For an assembly plant, a comparable figure may be only 1 cubic foot of records; whereas in a purchasing department, the amount may be as great as 12 cubic feet, yet still qualify as an effective records-retention practice.

Cost is used by many companies to keep records-retention work within reasonable limits. Cost for labor and space will vary depending upon the particular location, but cost for equipment is relatively much more uniform. For this latter, an average cost figure is 25 cents per cubic foot of records stored. However, meaningful records-retention cost data should include labor not only for storing but also for finding, and the unit in which the cost is expressed must be meaningful. Cost per cubic foot of records, for example, may not be meaningful for some types of equipment, lineal inches are not appropriate for others, and number of records may be of little value because of the wide variation in type, content, and size of records.

Additional cost information that shows the need to control records retained is that it costs about $1,200 to create the contents for one file drawer of correspondence. Assuming 5,000 papers in one file drawer, one-fifth of them are letters produced at an average cost of $1 each (probably low) and the remaining papers carbon copies at a cost of 4 cents each, the calculations are:

$$
\begin{aligned}
1{,}000 \times \$1.00 &= \$1{,}000 \\
4{,}000 \times 0.04 &= \underline{\quad 160} \\
\text{Total} &= \$1{,}160
\end{aligned}
$$

Helpful ratios can also be derived. To illustrate, a "usage" ratio reveals the extent to which the materials stored are being used. The formula is:

$$
\text{Usage ratio (in \%)} = \frac{\text{Requests} \times 100}{\text{References filed}}
$$

For example, if last month, 200 requests were made from 20,000 items stored, the usage ratio in percentage would be 200 × 100 divided by 20,000 or 1 percent. This ratio for stored materials will seldom exceed 5 percent. For active materials in the office files, it should run about 15–20 percent. Further analysis of usage ratios can be made, taking into account the rate of reference by type of record versus the age of the record. Such studies assist in better controlling of records-retention efforts.

Another ratio is the "accuracy" ratio, which is calculated by this formula:

$$
\text{Accuracy ratio (in \%)} = \frac{\text{Number of items not found} \times 100}{\text{Number of items found}}
$$

For 10 items not found and 10,000 found, the ratio is 0.1 percent. For a rating of excellent, the accuracy ratio should not be greater than 0.5 percent. A value of 3 percent or more signifies that remedial action is required. The accuracy ratio can be used for either active only, inactive only, or all stored records.

CHAPTER NINE

HANDLING OFFICE

SUPPLIES

Some desire is necessary to keep life in motion.
—*Samuel Johnson*

IMPORTANT, but sometimes neglected, is the handling of office supplies. They are used by all office personnel, both management and nonmanagement members. Since supplies are in such common use an attitude of indifference over their handling is not unusual. Their importance is often recognized only when unavailable or out of stock, for office employees must have proper supplies if maximum productivity is to be attained. The lack of the proper order pad, envelope, rubber stamp, or letterhead might cause delay in getting out important office work.

In addition, supplies represent an investment of capital. An office of 100 employees might easily have $10,000 worth of office supplies on hand; and unless properly looked after, deterioration and waste take place. And supplies cost money. Commonly they represent the largest nonsalary single cost item in an office. Studies indicate office supplies account for approximately 20 percent of the nonsalary costs. Assuming salary costs are 65 percent of total office costs, nonsalary would be 35 percent (100–65) and office supplies would be equal to 20 percent of this 35 percent amount, or 7 percent. This seven percent for supplies compared to 65 percent for salaries means about $\frac{1}{9}$ ($\frac{7}{65}$) of salary cost is equal to supplies cost. Or at an average salary of $4500 a year, office supplies approximate $500 per office employee ($\frac{1}{9}$ of $4500). This is a tidy sum. It gives meaning to the statement that adequate attention should be given office supplies so that they are handled effectively and their costs are kept in line. A savings of 15 percent, which is indeed nominal, means a gain of $75 per employee.

Unless reasonable managerial supervision is exercised over office supplies, it is certain that there will be extravagance, needed items out of stock, excessive prices paid for certain items, and obsolete material in the stock room. Simple but effective measures can be taken to alleviate these conditions. Basic efficiency demands that emergency purchases be kept at a minimum and that numerous trips to the storeroom throughout the day be avoided. The purchasing practices to follow, use of specifications, storeroom operation, keeping of records, and stressing waste control, are some of the key areas that will be discussed in the following pages of this chapter.

OFFICE SUPPLIES DEFINED

Office supplies is a term connoting many meanings—the concept is quite flexible, omnibus, and all inclusive. In many respects it has a sort of miscellany meaning. We can think of office supplies as being various papers and other expendable and nonexpendable items, of a popular-priced value, used in the daily operations of an office. Commonly included are articles such as letterheads, envelopes, memo pads, carbon paper, forms, typewriter ribbons, erasers, pencils, pens, ink, file folders, catalogue folders, binders, plastic binding elements, labels, cleaning fluids, indexes, rubber bands, paper clips, staples, rubber stamps, tape, and gadgets of all sorts. These articles, especially when viewed individually, may seem quite insignificant. However, when considered as a group, they assume more meaningful implications as indicated above.

Some prefer not to include office forms in the category of supplies. For example, they can be considered as an integral part of an office system or procedure and must be specially designed and controlled to meet the specific needs of definite work tasks. They are more special and important than, say, memo pads and letterheads, but like all supplies, they must be on hand when needed, in the proper quantity, and should be purchased at the right price. We are not concerned here with form design and control, preferring to think of these activities as more intimately related to systems and procedures work. However, from the office supplies viewpoint, every office form should have a number and a title to expedite ordering and stocking routines. Also, an acceptable specification for the size, weight, and quality of paper should be followed in replenishing the supply; and questions regarding the padding and packaging of the forms are pertinent points affecting forms as a supply item.

Gadgets have been included in the meaning of office supplies. These are the numerous and almost undefinable small devices and items used in offices to facilitate some specific operation or service, expedite a certain office method, or reduce expenditures of effort and time. The following are illustrative: hand units for making raised-letter labels; small auxiliary lamp units; charts for payroll calculation, for activities, scheduling, and progress; special labels for addressing shipping cartons; preparations to put on finger tips to sort or handle papers quickly; plastic mailers of all sorts; hand marking tools of many varieties; marking devices; office furniture cleaner; chemical cleaning and dusting cloths; and desk racks. There are many more, but these will sufficiently identify this category. Since it is easy to purchase office gadgets which subsequent events prove are really not needed, the following criteria are offered to guide decisions in this area. First, make sure you will use the gadget often enough to justify the expense. Also, does the gadget assist in accomplishing work that without it would be difficult, time consuming, or not practical of achieving. Third, is the gadget the best available for the intended work for which it will be used.

OFFICE SUPPLIES AND STANDARDS

To manage the handling of office supplies we need some means of identifying, in reasonably accurate and well-understood terms, what is being purchased and where it is being used, so that acceptable supplies, suited for the usage intended, are procured. For discussional purposes, consider carbon paper—an item with which most people believe they are familiar. There is, however, carbon paper and carbon paper. All recognize it as tissue paper smoothly coated with wax and carbon. But there are a great many weights, types of surfaces, hardnesses, thicknesses of carbon coat, colors, and sizes of paper. Which one should be purchased and used? To answer this question requires not only some knowledge of what carbon papers are available, but also information regarding what usage is to be made of the carbon paper. How many copies are needed; is an electric or standard typewriter, or pen or pencil to be used; and if a typewriter, what is the hardness of the platen?

The need for standards, as demonstrated above, leads to the development of specifications, i.e., statements of certain requirements of office supplies for specific purposes or applications. *A standard is something established by either custom or authority as a gauge of such things as quality, performance, and service of any factor.* A standard is a reference line; it may be thought of as a basis of reckoning, i.e., a basis of comparison. Most standards represent the best current knowledge of an item or practice formulated and accepted to meet the needs of present conditions.

The establishment of a standard does not mean that perfection has been reached. For example, a standard for carbon paper *does not* imply that paper meeting all the particular requirements of that standard is the best carbon paper obtainable, it may actually be carbon paper of an inferior quality. What the standard actually means is that paper of the stated attributes expressed by the specifications is the type desired and is satisfactory for the specific purpose in mind, taking into account such things as the type of equipment, the price range, and the desired finished product. Standards specifying a low grade are not uncommon, they simply reflect the belief that for the process and use to which the supply is going to be subjected, the low grade is satisfactory.

Experience shows that after a standard has been set, it is common to try to improve the standard and to move it toward perfection. This is as it should be, for progress is dependent in large measure upon improvements in standards. In addition, the setting of a standard seems to place a level below which future standards will not be set, that is, once a standard is set, changes that are not in the direction of improvement are discouraged.

Who sets standards? Associations serving as clearing houses for companies interested in these efforts. Since 1947, the American Standards Association, Inc., with assistance by the Administrative Management Society has directed efforts to the establishing of standards for certain office supplies which it is hoped will prove useful to many managers. The American Standards Association does not set standards; it provides the machinery whereby every group concerned in any project has a right to participate in the setting of the standards. Adoption of the evolved standards are voluntary, but the benefits of good standards are so great that wide acceptance commonly follows.

ADVANTAGES OF OFFICE SUPPLIES STANDARDS

The advantages of the use of standards for office supplies include the following:

1. *Provide a common basis for understanding.* Standards provide a common terminology, or a common language, between the employee and supervisor or between the buyer and seller. Through the use of standards, it is possible to determine exactly what is being discussed, purchased, and used.

2. *Encourage simplicity.* Standards tend to eliminate unusual and complicated office supplies. The very nature of standards tends to encourage the use of simple descriptions and easily understood terms. Also, wide usage encourages understanding of the standard.

3. *Reduce waste.* Standards help to determine definite requirements.

Losses resulting from obsolete and excess materials are kept at a minimum when good standards are employed and strictly enforced.

4. *Provide effective connecting links between the findings of research and the application of research results.* Standards serve as the contact points for the application of research findings. New discoveries and improvements are introduced via the standards, and in this manner, the beneficial contributions of research are utilized with a minimum of time and effort.

SPECIFICATION AND STANDARDIZATION

For office supplies the common ways of expressing standards are by written specifications or by a model. The former is simply a detailed statement of the requirements that must be followed or that must be met by the supply item under consideration. The latter, or model, is a typical sample or exact representation of a specimen of the supply considered standard.

When standards are set up and used for any particular supply, this process or action is termed *standardization.* For example, when a company adopts certain stated standards regarding the type of carbon paper it will use, the practice is known as standardization. A degree of uniformity is implied in all standardization. In many cases standardization deals with an entire industry, not with just one enterprise. Hence, the development of standards leads to writing precise specifications concerning attributes such as quality, cost, and use. These specifications serve as the basis for the purchasing and the using of office supplies.

PURCHASING OF OFFICE SUPPLIES

It is mandatory that supplies be purchased correctly, with regard both to quantity and quality, if proper handling of supplies is to be realized. The simplest approach would seem to be to permit designated responsible people of the office to buy what is suited for and meets the need of their office unit. There is usually some of this type of buying in most offices. But scattered authority and responsibility for purchasing results in waste of many sorts. Typical is the case of the correspondence supervisor who had been ordering supplies as she saw fit to do so. After the annual budget had been approved she ordered 25,000 envelopes with special imprint. Much to her surprise, another 25,000 envelopes were delivered several days after her order had been delivered. Upon investigation she learned that the mailroom supervisor, hearing of several direct mail campaigns to be conducted, had gone out and ordered the envelopes she believed would be needed.

Purchasing is a specialized activity and concentrating it in the hands of a competent person usually results in uniform practices, better service, and lower costs. This concentration helps develop the buyer's specialized knowledge of office supplies and skill in negotiating the purchase, such as locating the buyer, purchasing in best quantities, and at satisfactory prices. In addition, adequate records of purchases located in one place can be maintained so that quick reference to the data of previous procurements is feasible and can be used to guide future purchases. Furthermore, the office manager, office supervisors, and other management members are permitted to ply their respective primary managerial activities. They are not interrupted by interviews with vendors' representatives, and forced to make decisions on matters about which they may not have the complete facts.

The purchasing function normally includes authority for determining possible vendors for each supply, securing quotations, comparing values and prices, establishing purchasing policies, placing the purchase orders, following-up, and maintaining purchasing records. In many instances the purchasing agent also assists in preparing the detailed specifications for the supply desired, possibly being aided in this work either by a standards committee, or by users of the product being bought. In other words, the usual relationship is to have the purchasing agent concentrate on making contacts with vendors and on entering into purchasing commitments. He buys the needed quantity and quality at the right price and time. The role of guidance on what supplies to purchase, expressed by specifications, is performed by others intimately concerned with the use of the purchased supply. The purchasing agent, however, normally offers his unique help from his market vantage point by offering practical suggestions to those drawing up the specifications.

THE PURCHASING PROCEDURE

In the interest of simplicity and for purposes here, it can be stated that purchasing supplies consists mainly of four general routines: (1) the request for purchase, (2) the request for quotation, (3) the issuing of the purchase order, and (4) the writing of receiving information that the supplies have been received. Each of these is important and each requires paperwork in the carrying out of its particular mission.

The request for purchase is manifest by a form written by an authorized person to ask the purchasing agent to buy supplies specified. This is referred to as a purchasing requisition. For stock items, it usually is prepared by the supplies storekeeper or whoever does this work, and for nonstock items by the supervisor or department head requesting the supplies. Purchasing requisitions are commonly written in duplicate, the original being sent to the purchasing agent, the other being retained by the person initiating the request. A traveling requisition can also be used and is very effective and practical. When storeroom records indicate a reorder is needed, the card for this item is removed from the storeroom file and sent to the purchasing agent. By this means, rewriting of data is eliminated and a listing of the order and usage of the item is supplied. Figure 90 shows a traveling requisition card. Note the information provided includes item number, description, vendor's terms and quotation, and complete data on stock, purchases, and receipts. The purchasing agent prepares his purchase order from this card, enters pertinent data thereon, and returns it to the storeskeeper.

In the interest of economy, purchase requisitions should be originated on some regularly scheduled basis. By consolidating requests and achieving best buying quantities, the number of purchase orders can be held to a minimum and ample time gained to locate the best purchase price and value being considered. Not only must the economical lot ordering quantity be given consideration, but also the inventory on hand, the rate of use, and the probability of continued usage, i.e., whether obsolescence or revisions will render the supplies less useful. The challenge is to establish realistic maximum and minimum quantities for each item, as well as the ordering point. These can be based on judgment guided by past experience. The analysis of the requirements for each item will help attain a balanced inventory of supplies. As a normal practice, it is usually best to buy small quantities at frequent intervals. For each item, the amount purchased should be in line with the rate of consumption, the time required to receive a replenishment from the supplier, the quantity considered minimal for the functioning of effective management, and the savings in cost, if any, which are achieved through larger quantity purchases of the item. Some companies find it desirable to carry a one-, two-, or three-months' supply of the principal items. When delivery is made, a reorder with specific date of delivery is immediately issued in order to maintain an adequate and balanced amount of stock. Some companies put bulk items on contract purchase, ordering a six-months' total with deliveries released on a monthly basis. Substantial savings are claimed from this practice, especially for stationery items.

Past usage information is helpful, but some judgment enters into the decision of how much to purchase. Remember that paper takes on a yellowish tinge with age. Letterheads and printed forms can become obsolete—the company name or telephone number is changed, a new system is installed, or modifications in an essential procedure are made. A big bargain may be offered in typewriter ribbons, but don't buy too many even under

TRAVEL REQUISITION

ITEM NO.	DESCRIPTION	STANDARD COST PER M	ORDER QUANTITY	MONTHLY USAGE	PURCHASE REMARKS

VENDOR	TERMS	QUOTATIONS	PURCHASE REMARKS
A			
B			
C			
D			

STOCK DATA

STOCK ON HAND	DATE	QUANT.	DATE WANTED

PURCHASE DATA

QUANTITY REQUIRED ON THIS ORDER	DATE	PURCHASE ORDER NUMBER	QUANTITY	PROMISE DATE

RECEIPTS

DATE	QUANTITY	DATE COMPLETE

FIG. 90. A traveling requisition form for ordering office supplies.

attractive price conditions. In one case, a supply to last the entire office for three years was purchased but long before that time the ribbons had dried out so that they lasted only one week under hard usage.

The purchase order is issued to the vendor requesting specific supplies shipped within a certain period. Normally it includes all necessary instructions of buyer and seller, general conditions of purchase, listing of supplies ordered, and the signature of the purchasing agent. All expressions should be in readily understood terms that, if necessary, can be checked and enforced, and that are clear statements of what shall and what shall not be done. Customarily the purchase order is written in at least four copies distributed as follows:

Copy 1. To the vendor authorizing the purchase.

Copy 2. Retained by purchasing agent for his records and control.

Copy 3. To storeskeeper as evidence of purchase and for verification of receipt of supplies to purchasing agent and subsequently to accounts payable for checking of vendor's invoice and its payment.

Copy 4. Second copy of purchasing agent for follow-up purposes.

Some have found that a combined requisition and purchase order form works out very well. Designs vary greatly but separate copies provide for several quotations. Another copy becomes the purchase order.

The receiving information shows that the supplies have been received and whether they are proper as to count and quality. The incoming supplies are inspected and usually three copies of the receiving report are made, the first copy accompanying the supplies to the storeroom, the second sent to the purchasing agent for comparison with the purchase order, and the third copy retained by the receiving department for its records. Figure 91 shows a typical form for receiving records. Included are the time received, purchase order number, from whom received, means of transportation, the item number, quantity and description, along with a statement of condition in which supplies were received. In some companies, any defective supplies are noted on the receipt form, while others prepare a separate defective supply form designed to handle this particular situation.

Checking supplies against the purchase order must be performed with care. Omitted items should be clearly noted and deleted from the subsequent payment of the bill. Likewise, the identity and concept of defective, broken, torn, or damaged supplies should be resolved and a fair settlement reached within a reasonable period. Compare prices quoted to prices charged and verify extensions, additions, and discounts extended.

RECEIVING RECORD			
Time Received	Purchase Order No.		Returned Supplies
Received From			Prepaid
Address			Collect
VIA			Freight Bill No.

	ITEM NO.	QUANTITY	DESCRIPTION
1			
2			
3			
4			
5			
6			
7			
8			
9			
10			
11			

Condition of Supplies

No. Packages	WEIGHT	Received By	Delivered To
		Checked By	

Be Accurate and Complete	SNYDER CO.	No. A7291

FIG. 91. Effective form for receiving record.

Systematic attention to these details will save money during the course of a year.

THE SUPPLIES STOREROOM

The requisitioning, receiving, storing, and issuing of office supplies takes place within the storeroom operation which is actually the focal control point for effective handling of office supplies. The area may be a large room, a portion of one, or just a single cabinet set up in the corner of the office. Ideally the storeroom should be in a convenient space that is least desirable for clerical work. Be sure it is clean and dry. The area should be enclosed and kept under lock and key. In most of the new office buildings, the center area of a typical floor plan or "services area" includes a supplies storeroom. In others, it is adjacent to the receiving room where material-handling means are convenient. The storeroom should be managed by one person, the storeskeeper, or one group, the stores committee. Unless this concentrated authority and responsibility are followed, effective management of supplies is not attained. Commonly the storeskeeper is a member of the office services department because having proper supplies available when needed is vital to supplying the office services required.

Physically there can be more than one storeroom and indeed this is necessary in large enterprises. But the management of the storeroom or storerooms should be under a single head, and if feasible only one storeroom should be provided. The advantages of this recommendation are many, including, importantly, that close attention to inventories and disbursements is obtained and that maintenance of adequate stockroom records is encouraged. There are also the gains of more accurate forecasting of the needs of supplies, better utilization of labor, and efficient storeroom layout. In some instances these advantages are viewed dimly if the single storeroom is quite far removed from some who use its services. Frequently this latter disadvantage is greatly inflated, but if valid, storage cabinets can be located at key points and regular schedules maintained for disbursing the supplies. The point is that reasonable control must be retained at all times.

The equipment need not be elaborate yet it should be adequate to meet the needs. Using discarded and obsolete cabinets, desks, and tables from the office proper to equip the storeroom is foolish economy, if in fact there is any economy at all. A storeroom needs the best equipment to perform its functions efficiently. This includes adjustable open shelving, preferably of steel to reduce the fire hazard. Cabinets, a standing-height table on casters, desk, file, pallets, and a hand truck represent minimum requirements.

The storeroom layout should take into account the characteristics of the area such as size, shape, and permissible floor load. Since there is much movement in and out of a storeroom, adequate aisle space takes on a special meaning. Straight aisles at least three feet in width, or six feet if a main aisle, should be supplied. Locate main aisles parallel with the longest dimension of the room and side aisles at right angles to the main aisles. It is a good idea to locate aisles opposite windows to improve light and ventilating of storeroom. Easy access must be provided for fire extinguishers. Inflammable supplies should have special storage facilities removed from the ordinary supplies. Space for storage on pallets is needed, and also provision for a desk and file in order to do the clerical work of keeping storeroom records should be included. Ordinarily this clerical space should be adjacent to the entrance or exit to expedite control. Also, provide only one entrance and one exit to the storeroom.

Arrange the stock according to some orderly plan. Index all items by number or code, and have a handy reference available to locate any item quickly. Arrange forms by their numbers. Place heavy items on the lower shelves and light items on the upper shelves. If possible, the heavy materials should be stored so that only short hauls of them are necessary. Areas near the walls or next to columns normally are best suited for heavy loads. Items more frequently used should be stored in the most accessible location, thus minimizing work in handling them. Papers should be stored flat and should not extend beyond the edge of the shelf. Storage in the original container is usually satisfactory, but often packages must be broken to issue the quantity requested. Broken packages lead to damaged supplies. Hence, the practice of storing supplies of broken packages in steel or fiberboard containers has merit, for protection is thus added and waste due to storage handling and damage is reduced.

STOREROOM RECORDS

Records are essential in order to have a supply of each item always available, to reorder replenishments in time and in proper amounts, and to keep the investment at a minimum and compatible with probable usage. These objectives are fairly simple and records to help achieve them are of many varieties. Whether actions are triggered by cumulative data or an actual balance total, by items, by dollars, or by arbitrary limits depends upon the evaluation and wishes of those in charge of storeroom supplies in any given case. Included in the records maintained, however, should be data indicating when to reorder to maintain adequate availability, the amount to reorder, the sources of supply, the required delivery time, and all transactions in and out of the storeroom by item. This takes a lot of doing, as the old saying goes, and necessitates accuracy, constant vigilance, and a strong urge for orderliness and details. The inventories are constantly changing and for success one must strive "to keep on top" of these changes by proper and timely entries in the records.

A number of basic underlying approaches can be followed including (1) time limits, (2) dollar limits, (3) economic order quantity, or (4) minimum and maximum. In the case of time limits, an item or a group of items can be acquired during a definite period. How much to reorder is not precisely determined, but for items requiring a relatively long time to acquire, there is indirect control. If the acquisition time were 90 days, and the time limits 30 days, the item would be reordered in 3 (90/30) different lots. Not all items need have the same time limits although it is best to constrain the number of time limits to be used. Time limits are not difficult to establish and use.

Dollar limits restrict the amount of money spent for an item or class of items. In this respect it is similar to a budget. Limitation of physical quantity is loose unless a few high-priced items make up the bulk of certain dollar-limit classes. The mix of items within each class can vary considerably, yet be within the dollar limits prescribed. Price increases should cause an upward adjustment in dollar limits, but commonly such adjustments are not made. Also, the dollar-limits approach fails to signal when to reorder and how much. It tells when supply is depleted and when supply exists.

Economic order quantity (*EOQ*) reveals when and how much to reorder so that minimum total costs are incurred. It takes into account the preparation cost of one purchase order, the usage of the item, and the costs for storing and financially carrying the stock. Mathematical formulas have been developed to calculate *EOQ* and their use might give a false sense of finality to adequate inventory control. Of themselves, the formulas are valid, but they are based on assumptions that may or may not exist in the future when the purchased items will be used. For example, it is assumed that future consumption can be fairly well forecast, and that the cost of preparation and of carrying are known. Also the accuracy of future deliveries and vendor instability are further imponderables. Nevertheless, *EOQ* is extremely helpful and its use can be modified by judgments concerning the assumptions implied in the formula use.

The minimum and maximum inventory level control method or some adaptation of it has won popular acclaim. The objective is to constrain the inventory of an item between maximum and minimum levels established for it. For many items a 2-weeks supply (or any other time estimate based on judgment, rate of usage, and replenishment time) is determined. This supply is considered a buffer stock to prevent a "stockout," or being "out" of the item. Although mathematically it is possible to determine which is less costly—having the inventory or having a stockout—the amount of safety stock is ordinarily determined by judgment as stated above. The ordering quantity is the difference between the minimum and the maximum levels. When to order this quantity is the ordering point, which is greater than the minimum level by the amount equal to that used during the replenishment period. As the new purchase is being produced and delivered, the inventory stock is being reduced. When it is reduced to the minimum level, the new purchase amount arrives, increasing the amount on hand to the maximum level. Usage continues until the inventory is reduced to the ordering point at which level the process is repeated, i.e., another new purchase is released. This concept is illustrated by Figure 92.

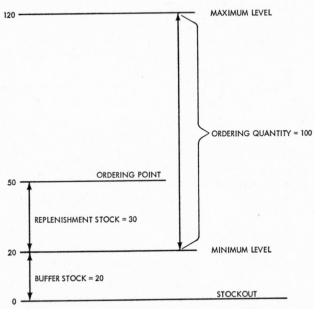

FIG. 92.   Illustrating the maximum and minimum levels approach to inventory control. With normal usage of 10 per week, and replenishment time required by vendor of 3 weeks, a 2-weeks buffer stock equals 20 (2 × 10), or the minimum level, and the replenishment stock is 30 (3 × 10), which added to the minimum level equals 50 (20 + 30), or reordering point. With an ordering quantity of 10 weeks usage, or 100 (10 × 10), the maximum level is 120 (20 + 100).

STOCK CONTROL CARDS

The design of the actual cards or documents on which entries covering inventory are made is subject to great variations. Also the equipment used must be taken into account. For a small number of items a loose-leaf binder or simple card file will suffice. These are portable, inexpensive, and adequate. However, where a large number of items are included, a visible card file with signals used to reveal the status of each stock item is very effective. A separate card is used for each item. Among the data recorded are the source of supply, the reordering point, the price, the date and amount on order, the amount on hand, the amount allotted or reserved for definite future uses, and the amount available.

Significant information about any selected record or records can be transferred to the visible margin of the card by codes of colored tabs positioned in this area of the card. For example, a red tab at the extreme right may indicate reorder level has been reached, or a green tab in the middle may signal an overstock situation or that more than the maximum level is in the storeroom. By scanning the visible margins of the cards, those items requiring attention can be quickly spotted and appropriate action taken on these specific items.

Figure 93 shows an inventory control card. The codes for signals in the visible margin are not shown. In this illustration the transactions or receipts are recorded as well as the requirements, or allocations. These have been placed adjacent to each other to reveal the immediate availability of the item. In addition the card shows the "current available" and the "on order." If the amount that is currently available is inadequate to meet a future requirement, a glance at the on-order column will show if more has been ordered, and if so, on what date, and in what quantity.

Another card design is shown by Figure 94. This card is filed vertically in a tub file. Cards are positioned in a shingled position so the extreme right column showing the amount of balance is visible for all cards. In this case a cumulative record and reference for quantities on order and received, reorder point, and unit cost are supplied. This type of card lends itself to many different designs and is very effective for storeroom records.

The time and the amount to reorder are derived from these inventory control cards. As indicated above under the discussion of purchasing, a requisition is sent to purchasing to process the item. However, other means to signal the time for ordering are followed. One such means is *bin-tag ordering point*, which in essence provides a signal for total replenishment of an item when a certain minimum of stock is reached. A record of the number of replenishments by months can also be kept. A bin-tag is

DESCRIPTION | ITEM NO. | COST | INVENTORY CONTROL CARD

TRANSACTIONS				REQUIREMENTS				CURRENT AVAILABLE		ON ORDER		
DATE	TRANS	QUANTITY	CUM RECEIPTS	REF	PERIOD	QUANTITY	CUM REQUIRE-MENT	PERIOD	QUANT.	DATE	P.O. NO.	QUANT.

FIG. 93. An effective specially designed inventory card.

ITEM NO.								
DESCRIPTION						MAX.		
						MIN.		
ON ORDER				DATE	ISSUED	RECEIVED	BALANCE	
DATE	REQUIS. NO.	QUANTITY	UNIT COST					

FIG. 94.   Control card for office supplies.

attached to the last package of the item, or near the bottom of the bin, so that arrival at the level indicated by the bin-tag signifies reordering is in order. The top portion of the bin-tag is then sent to purchasing and serves as a purchasing requisition. This portion has all the information imprinted on it that is needed for reordering. The bottom portion of the tag remains on the stored item to indicate that the purchasing agent has been notified to reorder. Large bright colored bin-tags can be used to attract attention and to avoid their being ignored or misplaced.

ISSUANCE OF SUPPLIES

In issuing requested supplies to employees of the office there is a great deal of merit in limiting the quantity issued at any one time to about a 2-weeks' supply. Large quantities of supplies encourage waste; too-small quantities involve excessive requisitions and trips to the stock room. Furthermore, too-large issuances frequently result in desks of employees being overloaded. Jamming several boxes of letterheads and envelopes in a desk drawer is destructive both to the desk and the supplies. The drawer becomes unsightly and may not work smoothly. The supplies become wrinkled, folded on corner, dog-eared, or torn.

It is also advisable to issue supplies only upon an authorized written request form which should be made out, in most cases, by the department head or by the supervisor of the unit receiving the supplies. File these requisitions and maintain a journal or record, by departments, of what is issued, when, and to whom. A periodic inspection of this record should be made to ascertain if consumption of supplies appears to be normal in the light of past requirements and the volume of work handled.

FIFO, or first-in first-out, should be followed. This means that the oldest stocks or what were received first are issued out first. This practice minimizes loss due to obsolescence, and damage from storing. Shifting stored items is expensive and undesirable work so a simple arrangement should be followed, with newly received stock placed on the bottom of the shelf or bin, and the old stock placed on the top and in the front so that it is issued first. Likewise supplies in mutilated packages should be used first to avoid possible further damage.

UPDATING STOREROOM SUPPLIES

Excess inventory, especially of slow moving or of nearly obsolete items, hinders efficient storeroom work. An excess should be identified as such and subjected to rigorous review. Checks should be made to reveal requisition amounts and authority, amounts purchased with requisition, overshipments, usage of item, and possible reasons for decline in demand. From such information, probable causes of the oversupply may be discovered and appropriate actions to avoid its recurrence can be taken. Excess inventory should be verified physically and segregated in the storeroom area. Disposition of the excess should be made within a reasonable period. Obsolete printed forms, for example, may be cut and packaged as scratch pads. Items that are unfit for any use should be discarded— either sold as scrap or destroyed by fire.

In other words, marginal stock items, such as infrequently used and slow-moving items, should be eliminated. Most office storerooms are burdened with such supplies which interfere with the smooth operation of the storeroom. Some companies have found that a periodic review of the stored items along with a study of the inventory records reveals items that have not been active for a long period. Decisions regarding such items should be made. Items returned to storeroom for repair should be sent out for repair or permanently withdrawn. Large stocks of returned materials should not be permitted to clutter up the storeroom.

In some instances, periodic campaigns to encourage employees to return unused and unneeded supplies have proven effective. This not only cleans up the desk and work areas, but it unfreezes items in one location for use in another location that needs the supplies. An inventory of all desks can be included in the campaign. While a bit dictatorial, properly handled it can bring excellent if not amazing results. Unless rigidly controlled, desks have a tendency to get stuffed with an assortment such as obsolete forms, a whole drawer full of scratch pads, two boxes of pencils, six erasers, and enough carbon paper to last twelve months.

MANAGEMENT OF OFFICE SUPPLIES

Most of what has been stated throughout this chapter is in the nature of managerial handling of supplies. Before closing this chapter, however, a few specifics might be added. It is recommended that all office supervisors be informed, by means of monthly statements, of the costs of office supplies issued to their respective units. These data can be quickly compiled from the requisitions for stock issue or from the journal of issues that is maintained. Such information accurately and regularly submitted helps to keep the supervisor conscious of the importance of office supplies, and the supervisor, in turn, will reflect this attitude to the individual employees. Some businesses follow the practice of charging the department for the supplies delivered and believe it to be an effective means of control. However, this practice must be handled very carefully, for some supplies become a part of the paper-processing cost and are not an indirect cost. Supplies are normally charged directly to "General and Administrative Expense" and any charging of the using department should be more in the nature of a record tallying than of a debit and credit balance accounting system.

It is effective to conduct a periodic follow-up to help insure that the supplies are needed and meet requirements. An effective practice is to select at random a requisition for supplies and investigate it thoroughly. Find out how the item is used, who uses it, whether it is best for the specific use, and whether the price paid for it is reasonable and in line competitively. Answers to these questions either will confirm that a satisfactory job of acquiring supplies is being done or will uncover areas which require remedial action. Also efforts should be made to determine if less-costly items could be substituted for certain supplies. Usually an arrangement providing for pretesting different products, or at least a willingness to try them out, is in order. There is a continual stream of new items and unless the time and trouble are taken to investigate them, the benefits they offer are never realized. Another suggestion is to keep a monthly record of the number of special or rush purchase orders or requisitions to issue stock that are processed. Although to some degree these types of orders appear necessary in the ordinary course of business, they commonly signify inefficiency and a cause of waste. The system and procedure followed should take care of the purchasing, receiving, storing, and issuing. Any service outside this program requires special attention and cost and of necessity should be held to a minimum.

Managers should supply the leadership to encourage employees to participate in campaigns designed to improve the handling of office supplies. Employees have practical and effective suggestions and in the final analysis they have a great influence upon the final achievements of any economy program. They should be encouraged to detect needs for improvement and to discuss new possibilities for progress, and not be completely absorbed in the routine chores of their immediate jobs. A machine turns out work effectively, but only a human being has the mental vision, imagination, and ability to make tactful suggestions for the improvement and better use of supplies. Informal surveys and studies of supplies will show whether waste is apparently getting out of hand. If so, an effective long-range remedy is to appeal to the employees to cease wasteful practices and help curtail needless expense for supplies. Contests, posters, and reminders are all worth while, but vital is the development within each employee of an attitude and a habit of using supplies wisely and purposefully. This does not mean to avoid using what is necessary or of being penny wise and pound foolish. The cardinal thought to get across to employees is: Use where the needs and results justify the expenditure and refrain from using supplies that have no justifiable purpose. Management backing, encouragement, and interest in identifying and promoting this thought are essential.